AMERICA'S MOST WANTED RECIPES

WITHOUT THE GUILT

Also by Ron Douglas

America's Most Wanted Recipes

More of America's Most Wanted Recipes

America's Most Wanted Recipes

Without the Guilt

Cut the Calories, Keep the Taste of Your Favorite Restaurant Dishes

Ron Douglas

ATRIA PAPERBACK
New York   London   Toronto   Sydney   New Delhi

This book features a compilation of recipes and cooking tips based on personal interpretation of the foods listed. Through trial and error, each recipe was re-created to taste the same as, or similar to, its restaurant/brand counterpart, but it is not the actual recipe used by the creator or manufacturer.

Several products displayed and mentioned in this book are trademarked. The companies that own these trademarks have not participated in, nor do they endorse, this book.

The brand or restaurant names for the recipes have been included only as an aid in cataloging the recipes and do not imply authenticity or endorsement by the creator or manufacturer. All restaurant and company names are trademarks of their respective owners. Please see the Trademarks section at the end of this book for detailed trademark credits.

Each of the recipes in this cookbook is adapted from or inspired by its restaurant/brand counterpart. For the actual and authentic versions of the food products listed in this compilation, please see the Restaurant Web Sites section at the back of this book and patronize the individual restaurants or manufacturers.

ATRIA PAPERBACK

A Division of Simon & Schuster, Inc.
1230 Avenue of the Americas
New York, NY 10020

Copyright © 2011 by Verity Associates LLC

All rights reserved, including the right to reproduce this book or portions thereof in any form whatsoever. For information, address Atria Books Subsidiary Rights Department, 1230 Avenue of the Americas, New York, NY 10020.

First Atria Paperback edition October 2011

ATRIA PAPERBACK and colophon are trademarks of Simon & Schuster, Inc.

For information about special discounts for bulk purchases, please contact Simon & Schuster Special Sales at 1-866-506-1949 or business@simonandschuster.com.

The Simon & Schuster Speakers Bureau can bring authors to your live event. For more information or to book an event, contact the Simon & Schuster Speakers Bureau at 1-866-248-3049 or visit our website at www.simonspeakers.com.

Manufactured in the United States of America

10   9   8   7   6   5   4   3   2   1

Library of Congress Cataloging-in-Publication Data

Douglas, Ron.
    America's most wanted recipes without the guilt : cut the calories, keep the taste of your favorite restaurant dishes / Ron Douglas.
        p.   cm.
1. Low-calorie diet—Recipes.   2. Cooking, American.
3. Restaurants—United States.   4. Cookbooks.   I. Title.
    RM237.73.D68   2011
    641.5'635—dc23   2011012512

ISBN 978-1-4516-2331-4
ISBN 978-1-4516-2335-2 (ebook)

Troy "Escalade" Jackson
January 11, 1976–February 20, 2011

CONTENTS

PREFACE

The *America's Most Wanted Recipes* cookbook series has become well known for providing accurate copycat recipes of your favorite restaurant dishes. People really love having the option of saving money by re-creating restaurant-quality meals at home whenever they want—so much so that we've developed a huge following, with more than 1 million books in print and over 1.9 million monthly views of our Web site, RecipeSecrets.net.

Now, in *America's Most Wanted Recipes Without the Guilt*, we've focused on providing reduced-calorie versions with the same great taste that you'll find at the most popular restaurants in the country. Yes, you can enjoy your favorite foods without the guilt!

America's Most Wanted Recipes Without the Guilt was inspired by my childhood friend and neighbor Troy "Escalade" Jackson, who passed away in his sleep in February 2011 at age thirty-five. Troy was a legendary athlete from Queens, New York, and had thousands of adoring fans and friends. He was a class act and will truly be missed.

In the wake of my friend's sudden passing, I decided to make *America's Most Wanted Recipes Without the Guilt* more than just a cookbook. I felt an obligation to use the success of my cookbooks as a platform for educating readers on how to eat more healthfully as a better way of life instead of as just a temporary diet.

We've enlisted the help of licensed, registered dietitian Mary M. Franz to provide nutritional details and healthy tips throughout this cookbook. We've also worked with Mary to provide you with a comprehensive health and nutrition guide, located at the back of this book.

For each recipe in *America's Most Wanted Recipes Without the Guilt*, we've included simple ways to make your favorite restaurant meals healthier, along with the number of calories saved by doing so. We hope that our examples help readers learn how to choose healthier options in their everyday meal planning.

THE OBESITY EPIDEMIC

It is no secret that Americans are getting heavier. Chances are good that you know someone who is struggling to lose weight, or maybe you are battling your own weight problem. If so, you know how incredibly difficult it can be to lose even a few pounds. And maybe, like many others, you have just given up and resigned yourself to living with your excess weight.

The facts are stunning. According to the Centers for Disease Control and Prevention (CDC), about 34 percent of American adults are either overweight or obese, and 6 percent are classified as "extremely obese." In addition, nearly 20 percent of American kids aged two to seventeen are now obese. Childhood obesity is of special concern because it often leads to poor health very early in life. For example, over half of obese kids have at least one risk factor for heart disease, such as high blood pressure or high cholesterol. In addition, children who are obese tend to be obese as adults.

People who are obese experience many negative effects on their health and well-being. In addition to having less energy and a poor self-image, obese individuals have higher rates of serious health problems, including diabetes, high blood pressure, heart disease, and some kinds of cancers, and experience physical ailments such as arthritis and back pain.

Reasons for Obesity

Why are we so heavy? There are many reasons for the explosion in the rate of obesity, but two of the main ones are an inactive lifestyle and poor eating habits. The past century saw a dramatic drop in the amount of exercise we get. Many jobs are now sedentary, in contrast to the active physical work such as farming that once employed most people. In addition, driving has replaced walking for nearly all of our errands and activities, so far fewer of the calories we consume are being burned. As for kids, cuts in school athletic programs, less outdoor play, and increased television-watching and video game use are to blame.

Our poor eating habits are just as troubling.

Skipping meals: Busy schedules and long commutes cause about 40 percent of Americans to skip breakfast; in addition, about one-third of people trying to lose weight skip meals regularly. However, missing meals, particularly breakfast, has been shown to lead to overeating later in the day, especially of high-calorie foods such as sweets and salty snacks.

Bigger portion sizes: If you eat out in restaurants, you have probably noticed that the amount of food on your plate is increasing. Your eyes are not deceiving you! Over the past twenty years, restaurant portions have doubled and tripled in size, resulting in hundreds, if not thousands, of extra calories. This so-called portion distortion (discussed later on) is thought to be one of the main drivers behind the obesity epidemic.

Eating more "empty-calorie foods": Empty-calorie foods are processed foods that contain large amounts of calories, fat, sugar, and salt, but little nutritional value. You know what they are: chips, cookies, cake, pie, fries, candy, soda, and doughnuts. Because these calorically loaded foods are now available on nearly every corner (from convenience stores, franchise coffee shops, and vending machines), we have the opportunity to eat more and more of them—and we do.

Not enough fruits and vegetables: Because fruits and vegetables are naturally low in calories and high in fiber, they fill us up and can help us lose or maintain weight. The U.S. Department of Agriculture *Dietary Guidelines for Americans, 2010* recommends eating 2 cups of fruit and 2½ cups of vegetables each day (about nine servings all together). However, less than 30 percent of Americans meet this goal.

Restaurant dining: Another possible reason for the increase in overweight and obesity is the number and types of meals eaten away from home. About 25 percent of Americans now eat fast food at least once a week, and many families have replaced dinners at home with take-out food or meals eaten at sit-down restaurants.

Although quick, convenient, and tasty, restaurant food tends to be high in calories, fat, sugar, and sodium. An average meal consisting of a cheeseburger, medium fries, and a medium soda in a fast-food restaurant comes in at around 1,100 calories, 50 grams of fat, and 1,300 mg of sodium, while a steak dinner with an appetizer and dessert at a popular restaurant chain can rack up 2,000 calories, over 100 grams of fat, and 4,000 mg of sodium. Such numbers are surprising even to veteran nutritionists, including Marion Nestle, professor of nutrition, food studies, and public health at New York University, who finds the sky-high calorie counts in restaurant foods to be "astonishing." "For someone like me who thinks that she knows about these things, I'm stunned by the number of calories in fast foods. I had no idea."

Why is restaurant food so fattening? The answer lies in the cooking methods as well as the ingredients that are used: butter, fats, oils, cream, cheese, heavy sauces, and sugar and other kinds of sweeteners.

One of the biggest culprits in boosting the calories in restaurant meals is fat, particularly butter, shortening, and frying fats, which contain high levels of saturated and trans fats. Because fat is a "flavor carrier" (meaning it enhances the taste and other sensory qualities of food), restaurant chefs often add it in large amounts to provide customers with the delicious dining experience they are seeking. Consider this: Nearly half of the fat in the aforementioned steak dinner is added during cooking, building in hundreds of extra calories.

Of course, fat is not the only culinary demon here. Soft drinks, shakes, and desserts are often loaded with sugar. A large fast-food shake may contain 145 grams (36 teaspoons) of sugar, pushing the calorie count to 1,100!

Fortunately, a new federal law now requires restaurants with twenty or more locations to post calorie counts for all of their menu items. This legislation was designed to help consumers make informed choices about what they are eating when dining out. Although many restaurant chains provide this information on their Web sites, they must now list calorie counts right on their menus. However, it may take many restaurants some time (perhaps a few years) to get up to speed with this new law.

PORTION DISTORTION

Americans like big things, and our restaurant meals are no exception. Throughout the past twenty years, restaurant portions have doubled and even tripled, leading to sky-high calorie counts for many restaurant dishes. And although many of us have come to accept these enormous portions as normal, the truth is that a typical restaurant meal often provides enough food for two or three people. The National Heart, Lung, and Blood Institute (NHLBI) has coined a term for this phenomenon: portion distortion.

FOOD	20 YEARS AGO		TODAY	
	PORTION	CALORIES	PORTION	CALORIES
Bagel	3-inch diameter	140	6-inch diameter	350
Cheeseburger	1	333	1 .	590
Spaghetti with meatballs	1 cup sauce 3 small meatballs	500	2 cups sauce 3 large meatballs	1,020
Soda	6.5 ounces	82	20 ounces	250
Blueberry muffin	1.5 ounces	210	5 ounces	500

COMPARISON OF PORTIONS AND CALORIES
20 YEARS AGO TO PRESENT DAY

Source: www.nhlbi.nih.gov.

Our dinner plates have also increased in size, from 9-inch diameter to 12-inch diameter since 1960; and many restaurant plates are even larger than that. It's a no-brainer: Bigger plates mean more food—as much as 30 percent more than half a century ago—and with it, more calories. Unless we burn those excess calories off, we will store them as fat.

Here's what you can do to combat portion distortion:

1. Take the quizzes on the NHLBI Web site (www.nhlbi.nih.gov) to find out how much you know about healthy portion sizes, and how much exercise you need to burn off excess calories from oversize portions. Some of the answers may surprise you!
2. Avoid "all you can eat" buffets. They are practically an open invitation to overeating.
3. *Supersized* means just what it sounds like: a huge portion with out-of-control calories. Avoid at all costs, even if the price is enticing.
4. Split appetizers and entrées with a fellow diner. You will still be full, but not uncomfortably so.
5. Look for smaller-sized entrées on the menu. Many restaurants are beginning to offer these.
6. Make a meal of appetizers, known as *tapas* in Spanish. Combining a variety of small appetizers and side dishes can lead to a satisfying meal that is much lower in calories. In fact, restaurants that serve only appetizers are rapidly becoming one of the hottest dining trends.
7. Use a smaller plate at home and fill it with food. After a few meals, you will get used to the smaller plate size and probably won't notice that you are eating less food.

NAVIGATING THE RESTAURANT WORLD

If you enjoy eating out and would like to make it a healthier experience, the following tips and guidelines may be helpful.

Restaurant Red Lights

These descriptions of restaurant dishes are clues that they have been prepared with large amounts of fat, and should be considered deal-breakers.

Fried/deep-fried/pan-fried: All three terms mean that the food has been cooked in hot oil, butter, or another type of fat.

Creamy/creamed: Butter and/or cream has been used to make the dish.

Scalloped: The dish has been baked in a cream sauce.

Au gratin: The food, often potatoes or a vegetable, has been topped and baked with a crust made of flour, butter, and/or cheese.

Battered/breaded: The food has been dipped in egg or some sort of fat, and then coated with flour, a batter, or bread crumbs before cooking.

Smothered in: The term is usually followed by the word *cheese, sauce,* or *cream.*

Stuffed: This means just what it sounds like—the food has been packed with a high-fat or starchy filling.

Crispy: The food has been breaded or battered and then fried.

Drizzled: The surface of the food has been covered with a layer of sauce, oil, or melted butter.

Restaurant Green Lights

The following cooking methods are lowest in added fats and may greatly reduce the calories in a restaurant meal.

Steamed: Cooked over hot steam from boiling water.

Poached: Covered and cooked in a liquid, usually broth, wine, or juice.

Seared: Usually refers to meat; means that it has been cooked very quickly over very high heat with little or no added fat; done to seal in juices and flavor.

Broiled: Cooked directly under very high heat, so that the fat in the food can drain away.

Grilled: Similar to broiling, except that the food is cooked directly above the heat source, usually coal or wood.

Sautéed/stir-fried: Cooked quickly over high heat in a very small amount of oil.

Roasted: Often refers to meat, but sometimes vegetables; the food has been cooked uncovered in a hot oven.

Braised/simmered: Cooked covered in a small amount of liquid.

In addition to checking out the way a restaurant meal is prepared, you can use the following strategies to help lower the amount of calories you consume when you eat out:

Ask for all sauces and dressings to be served on the side, and use them sparingly. Use a teaspoon (not a tablespoon) to add them to the food. And because the creamier ones are higher in fat and calories, it's best to opt for marinara (tomato) instead of cheese or cream sauce, and vinaigrette or olive oil dressing instead of ranch or the blue cheese type.

Skip the dinner rolls (you don't begin dinner at home with them, do you?), or ask your server to bring only a few, instead of a whole basket.

Be aware of the calories you drink. Alcohol contains nearly as many calories as fat, and when combined with juice, soda, or other mixers, it may contain as many calories as a dessert. Did you know that a frozen margarita made with 2 ounces of tequila and 4½ ounces of cocktail mix can have over 250 calories? By comparison, a 6-ounce glass of wine contains less than 130 calories. If you are a nondrinker, skip that 16-ounce soda and ask for water with lemon or flavored seltzer water instead.

Order a plain baked potato instead of fries. The humble potato is actually not that high in calories (a medium one has about 150 calories); however, once it is plunged into a vat of oil, the calorie count doubles.

Split the dessert with a friend. I know, you want to eat the *whole* thing yourself. But chances are you will feel that you have had enough by the time you've eaten half.

Finally, here are some healthy but tasty suggestions for ordering out:

Appetizers and Sides
- Grilled shrimp/shrimp cocktail
- Steamed clams or mussels
- Roasted or grilled vegetables with olive oil
- Raw vegetables with hummus (on the side)
- A cup of minestrone soup, gazpacho, or chili
- Fruit or vegetable salad
- A side order of steamed rice

Entrées
- Grilled chicken or beef skewers
- Pasta with marinara or primavera sauce
- Broiled salmon or tuna steak
- Chicken fajitas (without cheese)
- Marinated turkey tips

Desserts
- Fruit crisp
- Plain cake topped with fruit
- Low-fat ice cream, sherbet, mousse, or frozen yogurt

THE BENEFITS OF COOKING AT HOME

We have seen that restaurant meals are often high in "bad" fat, sugar, salt, and calories. And even healthier restaurant entrées can offer portions that are two and three times larger than we need.

One way to avoid the pitfalls of restaurant eating is to cook more at home. This may seem obvious, but for many busy on-the-go families, sitting down to a home-prepared meal is becoming a thing of the past. For many working parents, getting a meal on the table after a hectic day at the office seems like an impossible task. But it doesn't have to be. There are many simple, delicious, and easy meals that can be prepared in 30 minutes or less. The recipes in this cookbook will help you find great meals that are just right for you and your family.

There are many benefits to cooking at home. Here are some of the main ones:

- You can control the amounts of fat, salt, and sugar that you cook and season food with.
- You can choose healthier types of fat for cooking and baking, like olive and canola oils.
- You can tailor the dishes you make to meet special dietary needs of family members. For example, you can use less salt to accommodate someone on a low-sodium diet.
- You can use the freshest ingredients available and choose from locally grown produce.
- You can avoid the additives, preservatives, and other unnecessary ingredients that are often found in restaurant and convenience foods.
- You can give children hands-on cooking lessons. Kids who are introduced to cooking at an early age are more likely to have a better appreciation of food and nutrition.

- Cooking at home also provides you with endless opportunities for preparing creative and healthy meals. You can make sure that the meals you prepare are nutritionally superior (as well as tasty) by choosing your ingredients wisely and making healthy substitutions whenever possible.

The following suggestions are tried-and-true substitutions that will help lower the calories, fat, and sugar in the dishes you prepare at home.

Eggs: Use 2 egg whites instead of 1 whole egg. You can also substitute 2 teaspoons of ground flaxseed mixed with 2 to 3 tablespoons of water for 1 egg in baked goods. Simmer the flaxseed and water until the mixture takes on a gummy egglike texture, and let cool before mixing with other ingredients. Generally, you can substitute half of the eggs in a recipe without sacrificing flavor or texture.

Butter: Substitute an equal amount of canola oil for the butter. This works well for most recipes.

Butter, oil, and other fats: You can substitute an equal amount of applesauce or mashed banana for the fat in baked goods; for example, 1 tablespoon of applesauce can replace 1 tablespoon of butter or oil. For some recipes, like spice and chocolate cakes, an equal amount of canned pumpkin will also work. As with eggs, it is best to replace only one half of the fat in a recipe with fruit, since a certain amount of fat is needed for tenderness and flavor.

Cream: Use an equal amount of evaporated skim milk.

Sour cream: Use an equal amount of low-fat or nonfat sour cream, or creamed low-fat cottage cheese. Plain nonfat yogurt may also be used, though it may give a slightly different texture.

White flour: Use ½ to ¾ cup of whole wheat pastry flour instead of 1 cup of white flour. Whole wheat flour may also be used, though it tends to give a somewhat drier and denser texture to baked goods.

Sugar: You can cut the amount of sugar in a baked goods recipe by as much as half without sacrificing taste. When cutting sugar, you can also add extra cinnamon to boost the flavor.

Unsweetened chocolate: Use 3 tablespoons of cocoa powder for every ounce of unsweetened chocolate in a recipe.

Marinades for meat, fish, and vegetables: Cut the amount of oil in half and replace with equal amounts of pineapple juice and chicken broth.

Cake frosting: Sprinkle cake with confectioners' sugar or top with crushed pineapple in place of frosting.

Cream soups: Use mashed potatoes as a thickener instead of cream or cream sauce.

Finally, for kids who are fussy about eating vegetables, try adding finely grated carrots or green peppers to spaghetti sauce, and simmer. The flavor of the vegetables will blend with the tomato sauce, and the kids will never know they are eating those hated vegetables!

AMERICA'S MOST WANTED RECIPES

WITHOUT THE GUILT

APPLEBEE'S
Baby Back Ribs

Three 1-pound racks pork baby
back ribs, cut in half
1 cup tomato sauce
¼ cup apple cider vinegar
1 tablespoon dark brown sugar
4 packets Sweet'n Low (or your
favorite reduced-calorie sugar
substitute for cooking)

3 tablespoons Worcestershire
sauce
1 teaspoon liquid smoke
½ teaspoon salt

1. Place the ribs in a large pot and fill the pot with enough water to cover the ribs.

2. Bring the water to a boil, reduce the heat, cover, and simmer for 1 hour, or until the ribs are fork-tender.

3. While the ribs are simmering, combine the remaining ingredients in a medium saucepan and bring to a boil.

4. Reduce the heat and simmer, uncovered, stirring often, for 30 minutes, or until the sauce mixture is slightly thickened.

5. Preheat the broiler.

6. Place the simmered ribs, meat side down, on a broiler pan.

7. Brush with half the sauce and broil 4 to 5 inches from the heat source for 6 to 7 minutes, until the edges are slightly charred.

8. Turn the ribs over, brush with the remaining sauce, and broil for an additional 6 to 7 minutes, until the edges are slightly charred.

Serves 3

NUTRITIONAL INFORMATION (PER SERVING)

Calories: 736
Fat: 54 grams
Protein: 87 grams
Carbohydrates: 18 grams
Dietary Fiber: 1.2 grams

The original Applebee's version has 862 calories per serving. By using tomato sauce instead of ketchup and using only 1 tablespoon of brown sugar, you save 126 calories per serving.

APPLEBEE'S
Chicken Quesadilla Grande

Two 10-inch flour tortillas
1 tablespoon diet margarine, melted
2 tablespoons chipotle sauce
4 ounces grilled chicken breast

Filling
¼ cup shredded low-fat Cheddar cheese
1 medium jalapeño pepper, chopped
1 tablespoon sour cream
¼ cup salsa

Extras
Diced tomato
Diced onion
Chopped lettuce
Minced fresh cilantro

1. Brush one side of each tortilla with melted margarine.

2. Place one tortilla, margarine side down, on a work surface. Spread the chipotle sauce over the tortilla.

3. Slice the grilled chicken breast and spread it evenly on top of the sauce.

4. Evenly spread the filling ingredients over the chicken. Cover the top with the second tortilla, margarine side up.

5. Brown evenly on both sides in a nonstick skillet until the filling is heated thoroughly.

6. Cut into quarters and serve with the extras as desired.

Serves 1

Calories:	732
Fat:	24 grams
Protein:	54 grams
Carbohydrates:	80 grams
Dietary Fiber:	4.3 grams

The original Applebee's version has 1,440 calories per serving. By using slightly smaller tortillas, diet margarine instead of oil, and low-fat cheese, and eliminating the bacon, you save 708 calories per serving.

APPLEBEE'S
Crispy Orange Chicken Skillet

4 boneless, skinless chicken
  breasts
1 egg, beaten
1½ teaspoons salt
½ teaspoon black pepper
1 tablespoon diet margarine,
  melted
½ cup bread crumbs

Glaze
1 tablespoon diet margarine
1 teaspoon minced garlic
1½ teaspoons grated orange zest
1 cup orange juice
½ cup hoisin sauce
Pinch of cayenne pepper
1 tablespoon honey
Salt and black pepper to taste

1. Preheat the oven to 350°F.

2. Cut the chicken into 2-inch pieces and place in a large bowl. Add the egg, salt, pepper, and melted margarine.

3. Sprinkle the chicken pieces sparingly with the bread crumbs, being sure all sides have some crumbs.

4. Spread the chicken pieces on a baking sheet that has been sprayed with cooking spray. Bake at 350°F for about 15 minutes, until the chicken is lightly browned.

5. To make the glaze, melt the margarine in a small pan and add the garlic. Sauté for about 1 minute, being careful not to burn the garlic.

6. Add the remaining ingredients and bring to a slow boil.

7. Continue to cook, stirring, for about 3 minutes. Reduce the heat and simmer until the sauce thickens.

8. Arrange the chicken on a platter, pour the glaze over the top, and serve.

Serves 4

Calories:	330
Fat:	5 grams
Protein:	38 grams
Carbohydrates:	5 grams
Dietary Fiber:	0.73 gram

The original Applebee's version has 2,030 calories per serving. By making the portions slightly smaller (6 ounces instead of 8 ounces), coating in bread crumbs, baking instead of frying, and using honey instead of sugar in the glaze, you save 1,700 calories per serving.

APPLEBEE'S
Deadly Chocolate Sin

Raspberry Coulis
1 pint fresh raspberries
4 packets Sweet'n Low (or your favorite reduced-calorie sugar substitute for cooking)

Cake
3 ounces semisweet chocolate
2 ounces unsweetened chocolate
3 tablespoons cocoa powder
3 packets Sweet'n Low (or your favorite reduced-calorie sugar substitute for cooking)

8 tablespoons (½ cup) diet margarine
1 teaspoon vanilla extract
1½ cups egg substitute (such as Egg Beaters)
½ cup packed light brown sugar
6 tablespoons cornstarch

Garnish
1 pint fresh raspberries
12 sprigs fresh mint
6 sugar-free cookies, crumbled

1. Make the raspberry coulis: Process the fresh berries in a blender with the sweetener. Strain through a fine-mesh strainer to remove the seeds. Refrigerate until needed.

2. Preheat the oven to 275°F. Spray the bottom and sides of 12 (4-ounce) ramekins with cooking spray and set aside on a baking sheet.

3. In the top of a double boiler, place the semisweet and unsweetened chocolates, the cocoa powder, sweetener, margarine, and vanilla extract. Set over simmering water and stir until melted and well blended. Keep the heat low so the chocolate and margarine melt slowly.

4. In a large mixing bowl, combine the egg substitute and brown sugar. Beat at high speed until thickened, 5 to 7 minutes. Reduce the speed to low and slowly incorporate the cornstarch, 1 tablespoon at a time. Turn the mixer back to high and beat until soft peaks form, about 5 minutes.

5. Using a rubber spatula, gently fold the chocolate mixture into the beaten egg mixture until well blended. Spoon the mixture into each of the prepared ramekins and bake for 10 minutes, or until a toothpick inserted in the centers comes out clean. Let cool, cover with plastic wrap, and refrigerate until ready to serve.

6. To serve, dip a dinner knife into hot water and run it around the sides of each ramekin. Invert the ramekin onto a serving dish, gently remove the ramekin from the plate, and spoon the raspberry coulis around the cake. Garnish each serving with fresh raspberries, a mint sprig, and a few cookie crumbles on top.

Serves 12

NUTRITIONAL INFORMATION (PER SERVING)

Calories:	225
Fat:	12.19 grams
Protein:	5.63 grams
Carbohydrates:	27.35 grams
Dietary Fiber:	4.46 grams

The original Applebee's version has 510 calories per serving. By using fresh raspberries, diet margarine, egg substitute, and some artificial sweetener and then eliminating the whole cookies and chocolate pieces from the garnish, you save 285 calories per serving.

APPLEBEE'S
Santa Fe Chicken

8 boneless, skinless chicken breasts
One 6-ounce block low-fat
  Monterey Jack cheese
1 cup Italian bread crumbs
1½ tablespoons grated Parmesan
  cheese
½ teaspoon salt
½ teaspoon ground cumin
½ teaspoon pepper

4 tablespoons (¼ cup) diet
  margarine, melted
1 tablespoon all-purpose flour
1 cup skim milk
1 small red bell pepper, seeded and
  diced
1 small green bell pepper, seeded
  and diced

1. Place 1 chicken breast between two sheets of waxed paper. Working from the center to the edges, pound the chicken with a meat mallet until it is flat and rectangular shaped. Repeat with the remaining breasts.

2. Cut half of the cheese block into 8 slices; grate the remaining cheese and set aside.

3. Wrap each flattened chicken breast around a slice of cheese; secure with wooden toothpicks.

4. Combine the bread crumbs, Parmesan cheese, salt, cumin, and pepper.

5. Roll the secured chicken pieces in 3 tablespoons of the melted margarine and then in the bread crumb mixture.

6. Place the chicken breasts in a 13 by 9-inch baking dish, being careful not to crowd them.

7. Refrigerate for 1 hour or freeze to bake later. (If you decide to freeze, you will need to increase the baking time by 5 to 10 minutes.)

8. Preheat the oven to 400°F.

9. Bake the chicken breasts for 25 to 30 minutes, until cooked through.

10. Place the remaining 1 tablespoon melted margarine in a saucepan, stir in the flour, and whisk in the milk. Bring the mixture to a simmer.

11. Stir in the grated Monterey Jack cheese. Reduce the heat and simmer, stirring, until thick.

12. Place the chicken on individual plates. Pour the sauce on top and garnish with the diced bell peppers.

Serves 8

NUTRITIONAL INFORMATION (PER SERVING)

Calories:	395
Fat:	8.5 grams
Protein:	10 grams
Carbohydrates:	13.5 grams
Dietary Fiber:	0.068 gram

The original Applebee's version has 520 calories per serving. By using low-fat cheese, skim milk, and diet margarine, you save 125 calories per serving.

APPLEBEE'S
Santa Fe Chicken Salad

Pico de Gallo
3 large tomatoes, diced
1 large onion, diced
2 tablespoons diced jalapeño pepper
2 teaspoons salt
½ teaspoon pepper
½ teaspoon garlic powder
½ cup chopped fresh cilantro
1 tablespoon lime juice

Chicken Marinade
¼ cup lime juice
2 tablespoons orange juice
¾ teaspoon minced jalapeño pepper
¾ teaspoon minced garlic
¼ teaspoon salt
¼ teaspoon pepper
1 teaspoon fajita seasoning mix
1 boneless, skinless chicken breast

Mexi-Ranch Dressing
¼ cup nonfat mayonnaise
¼ cup nonfat sour cream
1 teaspoon lime juice
1 teaspoon minced jalapeño pepper
1 teaspoon minced onion
1 tablespoon adobo seasoning

2 cups lettuce or mixed greens
¼ cup shredded low-fat Cheddar cheese

1. Make the pico de gallo by combining all the ingredients and refrigerating overnight in a tightly covered container.

2. Marinate the chicken by combining all the marinade ingredients except the fajita seasoning mix, adding the chicken, and refrigerating overnight in a tightly covered container, turning the chicken occasionally.

3. Make the dressing by thoroughly combining all the ingredients and refrigerating in a tightly covered container.

4. When you are ready to prepare the salad, preheat the grill to medium heat or preheat the broiler.

5. Remove the chicken from the marinade and shake off the excess liquid. Season both sides of the chicken with the reserved fajita seasoning mix and grill the chicken until cooked through.

6. Prepare a bowl with the lettuce. Slice the chicken breast into short strips and place on top of the greens. Garnish the top with the cheese. Serve with the pico de gallo and Mexi-ranch dressing.

Serves 1

NUTRITIONAL INFORMATION (PER SERVING)
Calories: 722
Fat: 27.43 grams
Protein: 65.79 grams
Carbohydrates: 57.95 grams
Dietary Fiber: 9.50 grams

The original Applebee's version has 1,300 calories per serving. By using nonfat mayonnaise and sour cream, and low-fat cheese, and eliminating the crushed tortilla chips and guacamole on top, you save 578 calories per serving. This makes a very large salad. Share it with a friend: Add another cup of lettuce and split everything else, and it is only about 375 calories per serving for 2 servings.

APPLEBEE'S
Spinach Pizza

¼ cup skim milk
¼ cup all-purpose flour
⅓ cup nutritional yeast
One 10-ounce package frozen
  spinach, thawed and squeezed
1 medium onion, chopped
4 cloves garlic, minced
1 tablespoon olive oil

5 medium plum tomatoes,
  roughly chopped
8 ounces mushrooms, sliced
1 teaspoon dried basil
1 teaspoon parsley flakes
1 teaspoon cayenne pepper
6 slices Sara Lee diet wheat bread
½ cup low-fat Parmesan cheese

1. Heat the skim milk in a large saucepan until hot but not boiling.

2. Stir in the flour and continue stirring until the sauce begins to thicken.

3. Reduce the heat and add the nutritional yeast and spinach.

4. Stir constantly until the sauce is thick and gooey, 3 to 4 minutes.

5. In a large skillet, sauté the onion and garlic in the oil until the onion is tender.

6. Stir in the tomatoes, mushrooms, herbs, and cayenne. Cook, stirring, until heated through. Drain off any liquid.

7. Preheat the oven to 425°F.

8. Remove the crust from each of the slices of bread. Using a rolling pin, roll the slices flat.

9. Place the bread on a cookie sheet or pizza pan.

10. Spread the spinach sauce evenly over each slice.

11. Top with the tomato mixture.

12. Sprinkle with the cheese.

13. Bake for 5 to 7 minutes, until the cheese is melted.

Serves 3

Calories: 315
Fat: 10.78 grams
Protein: 20.86 grams
Carbohydrates: 38.14 grams
Dietary Fiber: 8.75 grams

The original Applebee's version has 420 calories per serving. By using low-fat cheese, skim milk instead of rice milk, and diet bread in place of the pitas, you save 105 calories per serving.

BAHAMA BREEZE
Jamaican Jerk Grilled Chicken

Jamaican Marinade
¼ cup olive oil
2 tablespoons Jamaican jerk
  seasoning
¼ cup orange juice
¼ cup rice wine vinegar
1 tablespoon dark Jamaican rum
½ cup chopped red onion
½ teaspoon Cajun blackening spice
1 tablespoon dried oregano
3 green onions, chopped

Juice of 1 lime
1 habanero pepper, seeded and
  minced
¼ cup chopped garlic
1 tablespoon chopped fresh thyme
1 teaspoon ground allspice
1 cup water

3 pounds boneless, skinless chicken
  breasts
Jamaican jerk seasoning

1. Place all the Jamaican marinade ingredients in a large bowl and mix to evenly combine.

2. Cut the chicken crosswise into 3 by 2-inch strips. Add to the marinade, stir well, cover with plastic wrap, and place in the refrigerator. Marinate the chicken for 16 to 24 hours before cooking.

3. Preheat the oven to 350°F.

4. Remove the chicken from the marinade and place on a cooling rack placed over a cookie sheet. This will allow the chicken to drain so the jerk seasoning will adhere. Discard the marinade.

5. Rub the chicken with the Jamaican jerk seasoning and place on a sheet pan.

6. Bake the chicken for 15 to 20 minutes, until fully cooked.

7. Remove from the oven and let cool. Place in the refrigerator to chill.

8. Preheat the grill to medium heat.

9. Place the chilled chicken on the grill and grill for 2 to 3 minutes on each side, until fully cooked to 165°F. Serve hot.

Serves 6

Calories: 370
Fat: 14.92 grams
Protein: 48.63 grams
Carbohydrates: 3.16 grams
Dietary Fiber: 0.25 gram

The original Bahama Breeze version is for chicken wings and has 960 calories per serving. By using boneless, skinless chicken breasts, you have generous 8-ounce servings and save 590 calories per person. You still get all the flavors of the Jamaican jerk without all the extra calories.

BAHAMA BREEZE
Seafood Paella

8 ounces chicken tenders, cut into quarters

8 ounces jumbo shrimp, peeled and deveined

8 ounces jumbo sea scallops

8 ounces fresh fish, cut into 1-inch cubes

4 teaspoons Creole seasoning

2 tablespoons diet margarine

1 cup chicken broth

6 mussels, debearded and scrubbed

¼ cup green peas

3 cups cooked yellow rice

Fresh cilantro sprigs, for garnish

1. Season the chicken, shrimp, scallops, and fish separately with the Creole seasoning, using 1 teaspoon for each.

2. Melt the margarine in a skillet large enough to hold all the ingredients. Start with the chicken, sautéing until partially cooked through, then add the scallops, the fish, and the shrimp. Sauté for a few minutes, until the seafood is nearly cooked through.

3. Add the chicken broth and mussels. Simmer until the mussels open, discarding any that remain closed.

4. Finally, add the green peas and yellow rice, stirring frequently to make sure all the ingredients are evenly mixed. Serve garnished with fresh cilantro sprigs.

Serves 6

NUTRITIONAL INFORMATION (PER SERVING)

Calories: 292

Fat: 9.43 grams

Protein: 27.55 grams

Carbohydrates: 27.84 grams

Dietary Fiber: 2.32 grams

The original Bahama Breeze version has 585 calories per serving. By eliminating the chorizo, using diet margarine, cutting back on the amount of rice per serving, and making each serving a little smaller, you cut the calories in half and save 293 calories per serving. (Even with smaller servings, you have about 6 ounces of meat and ½ cup of rice in each serving.)

BENNIGAN'S
Baked Monte Cristo Sandwich

Four 1-ounce slices low-fat Swiss cheese

Four 1-ounce slices cooked turkey

8 slices Sara Lee diet wheat bread

¾ cup egg substitute (such as Egg Beaters)

⅔ cup skim milk

1 envelope onion soup mix

3 tablespoons diet margarine

Dijon Mustard Dipping Sauce

½ cup nonfat sour cream

2 tablespoons skim milk

1 tablespoon Dijon mustard

1. Preheat the oven to 450°F.

2. Place 1 slice of cheese and 1 slice of turkey on each of 4 bread slices. Top each with another slice of bread to make 4 sandwiches.

3. In a pie plate, mix the egg substitute, milk, and onion soup mix until well blended. Dip each sandwich into the egg mixture, spooning the onion pieces onto the bread.

4. Make sure all the egg mixture is used. Place the margarine in a 15 by 10-inch jelly roll pan. Set the pan in the oven for about 2 minutes to melt the margarine.

5. Carefully place the sandwiches in the pan and drizzle any remaining egg mixture over them. Bake for 5 minutes. Carefully turn the sandwiches over and continue baking until golden brown.

6. Prepare the dipping sauce: In a bowl, combine the sour cream, milk, and mustard. Mix well and then chill until ready to serve.

Serves 4

Calories: 310
Fat: 8.58 grams
Protein: 25.66 grams
Carbohydrates: 25.43 grams
Dietary Fiber: 2.05 grams

The original Bennigan's version has 643 calories per serving. By using low-fat cheese, diet bread, diet margarine, egg substitute, skim milk, and nonfat sour cream, you save 333 calories per serving.

BOSTON MARKET
Macaroni and Cheese

1 tablespoon minced onion
2 tablespoons diet margarine, melted
¼ cup all-purpose flour
2 cups skim milk
4 ounces low-fat American cheese, cubed
¼ cup cubed low-fat Cheddar cheese

2 tablespoons low-fat blue cheese dressing
1 teaspoon salt
Pinch of pepper
¼ teaspoon dry mustard
4 ounces macaroni or pasta of choice

1. Preheat the oven to 400°F.
2. In a large saucepan, sauté the onion in the margarine until translucent.
3. Stir in the flour and cook for 2 minutes.
4. Slowly stir in the milk.
5. Stir in the cheeses, blue cheese dressing, salt, pepper, and mustard.
6. Continue to cook over medium heat, stirring constantly, until thickened.
7. Meanwhile, cook the macaroni until al dente. Stir the drained macaroni into the sauce.
8. Spray a casserole dish with cooking spray and pour the pasta mixture into the dish.
9. Bake for 20 minutes.

Serves 4

Calories: 260
Fat: 5.04 grams
Protein: 17.5 grams
Carbohydrates: 36.32 grams
Dietary Fiber: 1.35 grams

The original Boston Market version has 300 calories per serving. By using skim milk and low-fat cheese, you save 40 calories per serving.

BOSTON MARKET
Meat Loaf

½ cup tomato sauce
1 tablespoon yellow mustard
1 tablespoon light brown sugar
3 slices Sara Lee diet wheat bread,
toasted until crisp
1½ pounds extra-lean ground beef
(95% lean)

⅓ cup all-purpose flour
¾ teaspoon salt
½ teaspoon onion powder
¼ teaspoon pepper
2 cloves garlic, minced
1 egg, beaten

1. Preheat the oven to 400°F.

2. In a large bowl, stir together the tomato sauce, mustard, and brown sugar. Set aside ¼ cup of the mixture for a topping.

3. Crumble the toasted bread into bread crumbs.

4. Mix the bread crumbs, beef, flour, salt, onion powder, pepper, garlic, egg, and tomato sauce mixture together thoroughly. (Your hands will do this most efficiently.)

5. Form the mixture into a loaf and place in a 9 by 5-inch loaf pan that has been sprayed with cooking spray.

6. Bake, covered, for 30 minutes.

7. Uncover the loaf and drain the fat from the pan. Slice the meat loaf into 6 slices while still in the pan.

8. Drizzle the reserved tomato sauce mixture evenly over the meat loaf.

9. Bake, uncovered, for an additional 30 minutes, or until cooked through.

Serves 6

Calories: 224
Fat: 6.62 grams
Protein: 27.7 grams
Carbohydrates: 6.9 grams
Dietary Fiber: 0.92 gram

The original Boston Market version has 480 calories per serving. By using tomato sauce instead of ketchup, very lean ground beef, and diet bread crumbs instead of traditional bread crumbs, you save 256 calories per serving.

BOSTON MARKET
Vegetable Stuffing

2 large carrots, sliced
I pound mushrooms, sliced
One 14-ounce can chicken broth
2 ribs celery, cut into 5 pieces each
I tablespoon rubbed sage
½ teaspoon poultry seasoning
I tablespoon chicken bouillon
powder
3 tablespoons diet margarine,
melted

3 English muffins, cut into ½-inch
cubes
16 slices Sara Lee diet wheat
bread, toasted until crisp and cut
into ½-inch cubes
I tablespoon parsley flakes
2 tablespoons onion flakes

1. Preheat the oven to 350°F.

2. Place the sliced carrots and mushrooms in a Dutch oven.

3. Pour the chicken broth into a blender. Add the celery, sage, poultry seasoning, bouillon powder, and margarine. Blend for a few seconds, until the celery is finely minced.

4. Add the English muffin cubes, bread cubes, and parsley and onion flakes to the Dutch oven.

5. Pour the blender mixture into the Dutch oven and stir with a rubber spatula until completely moist.

6. Cover and bake for about 45 minutes, until heated through.

Serves 8

NUTRITIONAL INFORMATION (PER SERVING)

Calories: 170
Fat: 5.01 grams
Protein: 9.64 grams
Carbohydrates: 26.21 grams
Dietary Fiber: 3.46 grams

The original Boston Market version has 190 calories per serving. By using fresh vegetables instead of canned, diet margarine, and diet bread instead of traditional croutons, you save 20 calories per serving. (If you eliminate the English muffins and use an additional 6 slices of toasted diet bread, you cut another 20 calories from each serving.)

BUCA DI BEPPO
Chicken Saltimbocca

Four 5-ounce boneless, skinless
  chicken breasts
¼ teaspoon salt
1 tablespoon minced fresh sage
4 slices prosciutto
½ cup all-purpose flour
3 tablespoons diet margarine

½ cup white wine
One 3-ounce package fat-free
  cream cheese, softened
¾ cup artichoke hearts, quartered
¼ cup lemon juice
2 tablespoons drained capers,
  for garnish

1. Season the chicken breasts with the salt and sage. Lay a slice of prosciutto on each breast and pound it with the flat side of a meat mallet until the breast is a little less than ½ inch thick. Lightly dredge the chicken with the flour.

2. Melt 2 tablespoons of the margarine in a skillet and sauté the chicken, prosciutto side down, turning once, until golden brown on both sides. Remove the chicken from the pan. Deglaze the pan with the white wine. Add the cream cheese and whisk together until the sauce is smooth. Add the artichoke hearts with the lemon juice and the remaining 1 tablespoon margarine.

3. Let the mixture simmer until it begins to thicken. Taste for seasoning. To serve, pour the sauce over the chicken breasts and garnish with the capers.

Serves 4

NUTRITIONAL INFORMATION (PER SERVING)

Calories:	375
Fat:	11.23 grams
Protein:	37.95 grams
Carbohydrates:	25.54 grams
Dietary Fiber:	3.10 grams

The original Buca di Beppo version has 592 calories per serving. By using diet margarine instead of oil, and fat-free cream cheese instead of heavy cream, you save 217 calories per serving.

BUCA DI BEPPO
Chicken with Lemon

4 large lemons
Two 6-ounce boneless, skinless
  chicken breasts
Salt and pepper
I tablespoon all-purpose flour

4 tablespoons (¼ cup) diet
  margarine, melted
¼ cup chicken broth
2 tablespoons drained capers,
  for garnish

1. Cut 3 of the lemons in half, squeeze the juice through a fine-mesh strainer, and set it aside. Quarter the remaining lemon and save for garnish.

2. Preheat the oven to 325°F.

3. Season the chicken with salt and pepper and place on a baking sheet that has been sprayed with cooking spray.

4. Bake the chicken breasts for about 20 minutes, until cooked through.

5. While the chicken is baking, spoon the flour into a small skillet with 1 tablespoon of the melted margarine. Stir or whisk until the mixture is smooth and begins to brown slightly. Add the chicken broth and remaining 3 tablespoons margarine.

6. Continue to whisk the sauce as you add the lemon juice. As soon as the lemon juice is well incorporated into the mixture, remove the sauce from the heat.

7. Drizzle the lemon sauce over the chicken breasts and garnish with the capers and the reserved lemon quarters.

Serves 2

Calories: 248
Fat: 17.69 grams
Protein: 26.84 grams
Carbohydrates: 5.51 grams
Dietary Fiber: 0.60 gram

The original Buca di Beppo version has 295 calories per serving. By using diet margarine and baking the chicken instead of frying, you save 47 calories per serving.

CALIFORNIA PIZZA KITCHEN

Chicken-Tequila Fettuccine

1 pound whole wheat spinach fettuccine
1/3 cup plus 2 tablespoons chopped fresh cilantro
2 tablespoons minced garlic
2 tablespoons minced jalapeño pepper
3 tablespoons diet margarine
1/2 cup chicken broth
2 tablespoons gold tequila
2 tablespoons lime juice
1 1/4 pounds boneless, skinless chicken breasts
3 tablespoons soy sauce
1/4 medium red onion, thinly sliced
1/2 each medium red, yellow, and green bell pepper, thinly sliced
1 tablespoon nonfat sour cream
1 1/2 cups skim milk

1. Boil salted water to cook the pasta; cook until al dente.

2. Cook the 1/3 cup cilantro, the garlic, and the jalapeño in 2 tablespoons of the diet margarine over medium heat for 4 to 5 minutes.

3. Add the broth, tequila, and lime juice. Bring to a boil, then cook until reduced to a pastelike consistency; set aside.

4. Dice the chicken.

5. Pour the soy sauce over the diced chicken and set aside for 5 minutes.

6. Meanwhile, cook the onion and bell peppers, stirring occasionally, in the remaining 1 tablespoon diet margarine over medium heat. When the vegetables become limp, add the chicken and soy sauce. Toss and add the reserved tequila-lime paste, the sour cream, and the skim milk.

7. Bring the sauce to a boil, and boil until the chicken is cooked through and the sauce is thick (about 3 minutes).

8. Toss the sauce with the drained fettuccine and the 2 tablespoons cilantro.

Serves 6

Calories: 575
Fat: 10.07 grams
Protein: 40.5 grams
Carbohydrates: 34.34 grams
Dietary Fiber: 8.37 grams

The original California Pizza Kitchen version has 1,225 calories per serving. By making your portions slightly smaller (6 servings instead of 4) and using whole wheat pasta, diet margarine, nonfat sour cream, and skim milk, you save 650 calories per serving. (Even with smaller portions, each serving includes over 2½ ounces of fettuccine and over 3 ounces of chicken.)

CARRABBA'S ITALIAN GRILL

Chicken Bryan

Sun-Dried Tomato Sauce
1 tablespoon minced garlic
1 tablespoon minced onion
1 tablespoon diet margarine, melted
½ cup chicken broth
¼ cup lemon juice
1½ cups julienned dry-packed sun-dried tomatoes
¼ cup chopped fresh basil
½ teaspoon salt
½ teaspoon white pepper

Chicken
6 boneless, skinless chicken breasts
1 tablespoon diet margarine, melted
½ teaspoon salt
½ teaspoon black pepper
4 ounces fat-free Monterey Jack cheese, shredded

3 tablespoons diet margarine
One 3-ounce package fat-free cream cheese, softened

1. To make the sun-dried tomato sauce, sauté the garlic and onion in the margarine until soft. Add the chicken broth and lemon juice and simmer until reduced by half, 8 to 10 minutes. Stir in the sun-dried tomatoes, basil, salt, and white pepper, blending well. Set aside.

2. Preheat the grill to high heat.

3. Brush the chicken with the melted margarine and season with the salt and black pepper. Grill, turning once, until the chicken is cooked through and no longer pink in the middle. Remove the chicken to a serving platter. Sprinkle the cheese over the breasts and keep warm while you finish the tomato sauce.

4. Reheat the tomato sauce. Add the 3 tablespoons margarine and the cream cheese and stir to blend well. Pour the sauce over the chicken breasts and serve warm.

Serves 6

NUTRITIONAL INFORMATION (PER SERVING)

Calories: 295
Fat: 13.48 grams
Protein: 34.05 grams
Carbohydrates: 9.84 grams
Dietary Fiber: 1.77 grams

The original Carrabba's Italian Grill version has 540 calories per serving. By using diet margarine, no oil in the sun-dried tomatoes, and fat-free cheese, you save 245 calories per serving.

CARRABBA'S ITALIAN GRILL
Meatballs

8 ounces ground pork
8 ounces ground veal
8 ounces extra-lean ground beef (95% lean)
2 eggs, beaten
¼ cup grated low-fat Parmesan cheese

4 cloves garlic, finely chopped and sautéed
⅓ cup plain bread crumbs
¼ cup finely chopped fresh parsley
Salt and pepper

1. Preheat the oven to 375°F.
2. Combine all the ingredients in a medium bowl.
3. Roll the mixture into 1½-inch balls and place on a baking sheet.
4. Bake for 25 to 30 minutes, until the meatballs are cooked through.
5. Immediately remove the meatballs from the baking sheet and place on a paper towel to absorb any excess fat.

Serves 4

NUTRITIONAL INFORMATION (PER SERVING)

Calories: 395
Fat: 89.05 grams
Protein: 34.85 grams
Carbohydrates: 6.51 grams
Dietary Fiber: 0.55 gram

The original Carrabba's Italian Grill version has 700 calories per serving. Simply by using extra-lean beef and low-fat cheese and then baking these meatballs instead of frying, you save 305 calories per serving.

CARRABBA'S ITALIAN GRILL

Rigatoni Campagnolo

2 tablespoons diet margarine
8 ounces bulk turkey sausage
½ cup minced onion
1 medium red bell pepper,
    julienned
2 cloves garlic, minced
½ cup dry white wine
4 cups minced canned whole
    tomatoes, with juice

Pinch of red pepper flakes
Salt and black pepper
12 ounces rigatoni pasta, cooked
    until al dente
2 tablespoons julienned fresh basil
¼ cup grated low-fat Romano
    cheese

1. In a skillet, melt the margarine and sauté the sausage, crumbling it as you stir, until cooked through and browned. Add the onion and bell pepper and sauté until tender. Add the garlic and cook for 1 minute more.

2. Add the wine and simmer for about 3 minutes. Add the tomatoes and their juice, the red pepper flakes, and salt and black pepper to taste.

3. Bring the mixture to a boil for 1 minute, then reduce the heat and simmer until the sauce has thickened. Stir in the cooked pasta and toss with the basil and cheese. Simmer for a few minutes more, then serve.

Serves 4

NUTRITIONAL INFORMATION (PER SERVING)

Calories: 538
Fat: 12.22 grams
Protein: 21.65 grams
Carbohydrates: 81.49 grams
Dietary Fiber: 12.43 grams

The original Carrabba's Italian Grill version has 945 calories per serving. By using diet margarine, turkey sausage, and low-fat cheese, and reducing the amount of pasta per serving, you save 407 calories per serving.

CARRABBA'S ITALIAN GRILL

Stuffed Mushrooms Parmigiana

12 mushrooms, stems and caps
separated
2 tablespoons diet margarine
1 medium onion, minced
⅓ cup minced green bell pepper
1 small clove garlic, minced
2 slices Sara Lee diet wheat bread
2 tablespoons grated low-fat
Parmesan cheese

1 tablespoon chopped fresh
parsley
½ teaspoon seasoned salt
Pinch of pepper
¼ teaspoon dried oregano
¼ cup chicken broth

1. Preheat the oven to 325°F. Fill a shallow 13 by 9-inch baking dish with ¼ inch of water.

2. Mince the mushroom stems and sauté them in a skillet with the margarine, onion, bell pepper, and garlic. Sauté over low heat until the vegetables are cooked through and most of the liquid has evaporated.

3. Meanwhile, toast the bread until it is light brown and toasted all the way through, then crumble the bread into crumbs. Add the bread crumbs, cheese, parsley, salt, pepper, and oregano to the vegetables and mix well. Add the broth and stir to moisten the mixture. Remove from the heat and allow the mixture to cool enough to handle.

4. Fill the mushroom caps with the mixture and carefully place them in the baking dish. Bake for about 25 minutes, until they are cooked through.

Serves 4

Calories: 106
Fat: 6.20 grams
Protein: 3.60 grams
Carbohydrates: 12.81 grams
Dietary Fiber: 4.97 grams

The original Carrabba's Italian Grill version has 150 calories per serving. By using diet margarine, making your own bread crumbs, and eliminating the pepperoni, you save 44 calories per serving.

THE CHEESECAKE FACTORY

Banana Cream Cheesecake

Crust

Twenty 2½-inch square graham crackers

4 tablespoons (¼ cup) diet margarine, melted

Filling

Three 8-ounce packages fat-free cream cheese, softened

6 packets Sweet'n Low (or your favorite reduced-calorie sugar substitute for cooking)

2 tablespoons cornstarch

3 eggs

4 bananas, 2 mashed and 2 sliced

½ cup fat-free half-and-half

2 teaspoons vanilla extract

One 8-ounce container Cool Whip Lite

1. To make the crust, place the graham crackers in a blender; pulse until finely crushed. Add the margarine and process with pulses until thoroughly combined. Press the mixture onto the bottom of a 10-inch springform pan; refrigerate.

2. Preheat the oven to 350°F.

3. To make the filling, beat the cream cheese in a large bowl with an electric mixer at medium speed until creamy. Add the sweetener and cornstarch and beat until well blended. Add the eggs, one at a time, and continue beating.

4. Mix in the mashed bananas, half-and-half, and vanilla extract until incorporated.

5. Pour the cream cheese mixture into the chilled crust.

6. Place the pan on a cookie sheet and bake for 15 minutes. Reduce the oven temperature to 200°F and continue baking for 1 hour and 15 minutes, or until the center is almost set.

7. Loosen the edges of the cheesecake; let cool completely on a wire rack before removing the rim of the pan. Refrigerate, uncovered, for 6 hours.

Allow the cheesecake to stand at room temperature for 15 minutes before serving.

8. Top each slice of cheesecake with dollops of Cool Whip and the sliced bananas.

Serves 8

NUTRITIONAL INFORMATION (PER SERVING)

Calories:	285
Fat:	8.63 grams
Protein:	17.16 grams
Carbohydrates:	3.15 grams
Dietary Fiber:	0.9 gram

The original Cheesecake Factory version has 925 calories per serving. By using graham crackers and diet margarine in the crust and then using fat-free cream cheese, half-and-half, and artificial sweetener in the filling, you save 640 calories per serving.

THE CHEESECAKE FACTORY

Cajun Jambalaya Pasta

8 tablespoons (½ cup) diet margarine
2 teaspoons Cajun blackening spice
1 pound boneless, skinless chicken breasts, cut into small pieces
1 pound whole wheat linguine
½ cup clam juice
½ green bell pepper, cut into thin strips

½ red bell pepper, cut into thin strips
½ yellow bell pepper, cut into thin strips
1 small red onion, cut into thin strips
8 ounces medium shrimp, peeled and deveined
½ cup diced tomato

1. Place the margarine in a skillet over medium heat. Allow it to melt slightly. Add the Cajun spice to the pan and stir together with the melted margarine. Add the chicken to the pan and continue to cook until the chicken is about half done.

2. While the chicken is cooking, carefully place the pasta in boiling salted water and cook until al dente.

3. Pour the clam juice into the skillet with the spicy chicken. Add the bell peppers and the onion. Cook for another minute, making sure the vegetables are heated through and the chicken is almost done.

4. Add the shrimp. Toss the ingredients together and continue to cook until the shrimp are almost done.

5. Add the tomato to the pan. Continue to cook until both the shrimp and the chicken are cooked through.

6. Serve the pasta on plates or in bowls and top with the jambalaya mixture.

Serves 6

Calories: 400
Fat: 13.6 grams
Protein: 33.19 grams
Carbohydrates: 42.28 grams
Dietary Fiber: 8.37 grams

The original Cheesecake Factory version has 1,071 calories per serving. By simply using diet margarine instead of butter and slightly decreasing the portion size, you save 671 calories per serving.

THE CHEESECAKE FACTORY
Louisiana Chicken Pasta

Cajun Sauce
1 small yellow bell pepper, chopped
1 small red bell pepper, chopped
¾ small red onion, chopped
3 cloves garlic, minced
1 teaspoon red pepper flakes
1 tablespoon diet margarine
1 cup skim milk
One 3-ounce package fat-free cream cheese, softened
1 cup chicken broth
¼ cup julienned fresh basil leaves
1 cup grated low-fat Parmesan cheese
1 cup sliced mushrooms
Salt and black pepper

Chicken
3 slices Sara Lee diet wheat bread, toasted
¼ cup grated low-fat Parmesan cheese
1 cup skim milk
6 boneless, skinless chicken breasts, pounded to ¼-inch thickness

Pasta
1 pound whole wheat bow tie pasta, cooked until al dente

1. Make the Cajun sauce ahead of time by sautéing the yellow and red bell peppers, onion, garlic, and red pepper flakes in the margarine. Add the milk, cream cheese, and chicken broth and bring to a slow boil. Lower the heat and simmer until reduced by about one quarter. Add the basil, cheese, and mushrooms, then season with salt and black pepper. Simmer for a few minutes more, until the mushrooms are cooked and all the ingredients are combined. Let cool, then set aside or refrigerate in a covered container. Gently reheat the sauce when ready to use.

2. Preheat the oven to 350°F.

3. To prepare the chicken breasts, crumble the toasted bread into bread crumbs. Add the cheese to the bread crumbs. Pour the milk into a shallow bowl and dip each chicken breast in the milk, then in the bread crumb mixture. Place the chicken breasts on a baking sheet sprayed with cooking spray. Sprinkle any leftover crumbs on top of the chicken.

4. Bake the chicken for about 30 minutes, until done through the middle.

5. Toss the cooked pasta with the prepared sauce. Spoon the pasta into serving bowls and top with the baked chicken breasts. (You can leave the breasts whole or cut into diagonal slices for an attractive presentation.)

Serves 6

NUTRITIONAL INFORMATION (PER SERVING)

Calories:	531
Fat:	10.62 grams
Protein:	47.38 grams
Carbohydrates:	73.65 grams
Dietary Fiber:	11.63 grams

The original Cheesecake Factory version has 1,400 calories per serving. By baking the chicken in your own bread crumbs instead of frying, and using diet margarine, skim milk, and low-fat cheese rather than heavy cream and butter, you save a big 869 calories per serving.

THE CHEESECAKE FACTORY

Oreo Cheesecake

Crust

2 tablespoons diet margarine, melted

1½ cups sugar-free chocolate cookie crumbs (about 25 wafer cookies, finely chopped)

Filling

Three 8-ounce packages fat-free cream cheese, softened

¼ cup sugar

6 packets Sweet'n Low (or your favorite reduced-calorie sugar substitute for cooking)

5 eggs

2 teaspoons vanilla extract

¼ teaspoon salt

¼ cup all-purpose flour

8 ounces fat-free sour cream

5 Oreo cookies, coarsely chopped

1. Have all the ingredients at room temperature before beginning.

2. Preheat the oven to 325°F.

3. To make the crust, mix the melted margarine with the cookie crumbs and press onto the bottom and 1½ inches up the sides of a 9-inch springform pan; set aside.

4. To make the filling, beat the cream cheese with an electric mixer on low until fluffy.

5. Add the sugar and sweetener and continue beating the cream cheese until well mixed.

6. Add the eggs one at a time and continue to beat until blended.

7. Add the vanilla extract, salt, and flour to the cream cheese mixture and beat until smooth. Add the sour cream and beat.

8. Stir in the 5 coarsely chopped Oreo cookies with a spoon.

9. Pour the cream cheese mixture into the springform pan.

10. Place the pan in the middle of the oven and bake for 1 hour and 15 minutes.

11. After that time, prop open the oven door and let the cheesecake stay in the oven for 1 hour; do not turn the oven off. Remove from the oven and let cool. Place in the refrigerator for 24 hours.

12. To serve, run a knife or metal spatula around the sides of the pan to loosen the cake, and remove from the pan.

Serves 6

NUTRITIONAL INFORMATION (PER SERVING)

Calories:	442
Fat:	9.22 grams
Protein:	21.98 grams
Carbohydrates:	27.63 grams
Dietary Fiber:	1.42 grams

The original Cheesecake Factory version has 869 calories per serving. By using diet margarine and fat-free cream cheese and sour cream, replacing part of the sugar with sweetener, using a fat-free chocolate cookie in the crust, and eliminating the Oreo cookie topping, you save 427 calories per serving.

THE CHEESECAKE FACTORY
Pumpkin Cheesecake

Crust

2 cups crushed sugar-free sugar cookies

1 packet Sweet'n Low (or your favorite reduced-calorie sugar substitute for cooking)

1 teaspoon ground cinnamon

5 tablespoons diet margarine, melted

Filling

Two 8-ounce packages fat-free cream cheese, softened

1 cup fat-free sour cream

½ cup granulated sugar

1 tablespoon light brown sugar

8 packets Sweet'n Low (or your favorite reduced-calorie sugar substitute for cooking)

1 teaspoon vanilla extract

One 15-ounce can pumpkin puree

2 teaspoons pumpkin pie spice

½ teaspoon ground cinnamon

4 eggs, beaten

Cool Whip Lite topping, for garnish

1. Preheat the oven to 350°F.

2. To make the crust, mix the ingredients until crumbly. Pat into a 9-inch springform pan, forming the crust along the bottom and up the sides. Set aside.

3. To make the filling, beat the cream cheese, sour cream, granulated and brown sugars, sweetener, and vanilla extract with an electric mixer until smooth. Add the pumpkin puree and the spices and blend. Add the eggs one at a time and blend again until mixed. Pour into the pan over the crust.

4. Bake for 40 to 45 minutes, until the center is almost set.

5. Turn the oven off and leave the cheesecake in the oven for an additional 30 minutes.

6. Remove from the oven and let cool. Refrigerate for several hours, until the cheesecake cools completely and firms.

7. To serve, run a knife or metal spatula around the sides of the pan to loosen the cake, and remove the pan. Garnish with a dollop of Cool Whip Lite.

Serves 10

Calories: 241
Fat: 6.05 grams
Protein: 11.88 grams
Carbohydrates: 40.41 grams
Dietary Fiber: 1.66 grams

The original Cheesecake Factory version has 739 calories per serving before the whipped cream and nuts are put on top. By using sugar-free cookies and diet margarine in the crust, using fat-free cream cheese and sour cream in the filling, and replacing part of the sugar with sweetener, you save 498 calories per serving. (By using real sugar for part of the recipe rather than replacing it completely with artificial sweetener, you still maintain the good texture in the cake.)

CHI-CHI'S
Baked Chicken Chimichangas

½ cup chopped onion
2 cloves garlic, minced
4 tablespoons (¼ cup) diet
  margarine
⅓ cup chili powder
One 16-ounce jar Chi-Chi's salsa
¼ cup water

½ teaspoon ground cumin
½ teaspoon ground cinnamon
1 pound cooked boneless, skinless
  chicken breasts, shredded
Salt
Six 8-inch flour tortillas, warmed
1 cup low-fat refried beans

1. Preheat the oven to 425°F. Spray a rimmed 15 by 10-inch baking pan with cooking spray.

2. In a large saucepan, sauté the onion and garlic in 2 tablespoons of the margarine until tender. Stir in the chili powder, ⅔ jar of the salsa, the water, cumin, and cinnamon. Pour the mixture into a blender or a food processor and process until smooth. Pour the mixture back into the saucepan; stir in the chicken. Add salt to taste.

3. Working with one tortilla at a time, spoon a heaped tablespoon of the refried beans down the center of each tortilla. Top with about ½ cup of the chicken mixture and roll up the tortilla to enclose the filling.

4. Place the chimichangas on the prepared baking pan, seam side down. Melt the remaining 2 tablespoons margarine and brush on all the sides of the chimichangas.

5. Bake for 15 minutes, or until golden brown and crisp, turning every 5 minutes.

6. Serve with the remaining ⅓ jar salsa.

Serves 6

Calories: 317
Fat: 8.96 grams
Protein: 27.05 grams
Carbohydrates: 37.46 grams
Dietary Fiber: 4.02 grams

The original Chi-Chi's version has 420 calories per serving. By using diet margarine, low-fat refried beans, and smaller tortillas, and topping only with salsa rather than sour cream and guacamole, you save 103 calories per serving.

CHI-CHI'S
Salsa Verde Chicken Kabobs

One 16-ounce jar Chi-Chi's salsa verde

4 tablespoons (¼ cup) diet margarine, melted

2 tablespoons lime juice

3 cloves garlic

1 boneless, skinless chicken breast, cut into 1½-inch strips

2 cups finely shredded cabbage

1½ cups finely julienned jicama

1 cup shredded carrots

⅓ cup coarsely chopped fresh cilantro

Pinch of salt

Pinch of pepper

1 large ripe banana

1. In a blender or food processor, combine the salsa verde, melted margarine, lime juice, and garlic. Process until smooth.

2. Remove ⅔ cup of the mixture and set aside in the refrigerator.

3. Place the chicken strips in a resealable plastic bag; pour the remaining salsa verde mixture over the chicken. Seal the bag and turn over several times to coat the pieces thoroughly. Refrigerate, turning the bag occasionally, for at least 4 hours or up to overnight.

4. In a large bowl, combine the cabbage, jicama, carrots, and cilantro. Stir in the reserved ⅔ cup salsa verde mixture. Add the salt and pepper; set aside.

5. Preheat the grill to medium heat. Thread the chicken pieces onto eight long bamboo skewers. (Be sure to presoak the skewers in water for 30 minutes before using.)

6. Grill the kabobs over medium-hot coals for 5 minutes on each side, or until the chicken is no longer pink in the center.

7. Slice the banana lengthwise and grill for 2 minutes on each side.

8. Serve the chicken kabobs and banana on top of the cabbage mixture.

Serves 2

Calories: 442
Fat: 17.98 grams
Protein: 31.89 grams
Carbohydrates: 49.65 grams
Dietary Fiber: 8.01 grams

The original Chi-Chi's version has 650 calories per serving. By using diet margarine and only 1 banana for two people, you save 208 calories per serving.

CHI-CHI'S
Steak and Mushroom Quesadillas

Marinade

2 tablespoons soy sauce

2 tablespoons pineapple juice

2 cloves garlic, crushed

Salt and pepper to taste

4 ounces flank or skirt steak

¼ cup sliced red bell pepper

¼ cup sliced green bell pepper

¼ cup sliced yellow onion

⅓ cup sliced mushrooms

⅛ teaspoon finely minced garlic

1 tablespoon diet margarine, melted

Two 6-inch flour tortillas

½ cup shredded low-fat Cheddar cheese

½ cup pico de gallo (see page 11), plus more as needed

Shredded iceberg lettuce

1. Combine all the marinade ingredients, and marinate the steak for at least 2 hours prior to grilling.

2. Preheat the grill to 350°F.

3. Grill the steak to the desired doneness. Remove the steak from the grill, allow to rest for about 10 minutes, then slice thinly.

4. Sauté the red bell pepper, green bell pepper, onion, mushrooms, and minced garlic in the margarine until the vegetables are semisoft and have a light golden color.

5. Lay the tortillas over medium-high heat on the grill or in a large sauté pan on the stove top. Top one tortilla with the cheese, pico de gallo, sautéed vegetables, and the grilled steak. Lay the second tortilla over the top.

6. Allow to heat until the cheese has melted. Once the cheese has melted, remove the quesadilla from the heat and cut into quarters.

7. Place the quesadillas on a large serving plate and garnish with shredded lettuce and additional pico de gallo, if desired.

Serves 4

Calories: 145
Fat: 5.95 grams
Protein: 11.88 grams
Carbohydrates: 11.46 grams
Dietary Fiber: 1.14 grams

The original Chi-Chi's version has 332 calories per serving. By using low-fat cheese and smaller tortillas, and eliminating the sour cream and guacamole toppings and the *con queso* dipping sauce, you save 187 calories per serving.

CHILI'S
Baby Back Ribs

6 pounds pork baby back ribs

2 cups water

Sauce

1 cup white vinegar

½ cup tomato paste

1 tablespoon dry mustard

4 packets Sweet'n Low (or your favorite reduced-calorie sugar substitute for cooking)

1 teaspoon liquid smoke

3 tablespoons Worcestershire sauce

1¼ teaspoons salt

½ teaspoon onion powder

2 cloves garlic, minced

¼ teaspoon paprika

2 teaspoons lemon juice

1. Preheat the oven to 350°F.

2. Cut the rib slabs in half, leaving 6 to 8 ribs per section. In a large roasting pan, arrange the ribs evenly, then add the water. Cover the pan tightly with a lid or foil to prevent steam from escaping. Bake for 3 hours.

3. About 2 hours into the baking time, make the sauce. In a large saucepan, combine all the sauce ingredients. Simmer over low heat for 1 hour, stirring occasionally.

4. Preheat the grill to medium heat. Remove the ribs from the roasting pan. Discard the water.

5. Cover the ribs with the sauce, saving about 1½ cups of the sauce for later use at the table. Grill the ribs on the barbecue for about 5 minutes per side, until slightly charred.

6. Serve with the remaining sauce.

Serves 8

NUTRITIONAL INFORMATION (PER SERVING)

Calories: 780
Fat: 55.64 grams
Protein: 65.59 grams
Carbohydrates: 3.11 grams
Dietary Fiber: 0.25 gram

The original Chili's version has 960 calories per serving. By using artificial sweetener and making the portions slightly smaller, you save 180 calories per serving. If you were to divide the recipe into 12 servings (this would still be 8 ounces of ribs per person), the calories would be only 520 per serving and you would be saving 440 calories.

CHILI'S
Beef Fajitas

1 pound sirloin steak
One 4-ounce can diced green chiles
1 tablespoon onion powder
1 tablespoon garlic powder
2 cups water
1 large red onion

1 large green bell pepper
1 tablespoon diet margarine
Four 6-inch flour tortillas
1 cup shredded low-fat Cheddar cheese
1 cup salsa

1. Cut the sirloin steak into bite-sized pieces.
2. Place the steak in a slow cooker with the chiles, onion and garlic powders, and water. Cook on low for 6 to 8 hours.
3. Cut the onion and bell pepper into small strips; sauté in the margarine until tender.
4. Warm the tortillas in the microwave for a few seconds each.
5. Drain the beef mixture. Spread in the center of each tortilla. Top with the cheese, salsa, and the onion and pepper mixture. Roll up the tortillas to enclose the filling.

Serves 4

NUTRITIONAL INFORMATION (PER SERVING)
Calories: 401
Fat: 14.29 grams
Protein: 35.4 grams
Carbohydrates: 32.15 grams
Dietary Fiber: 2.2 grams

The original Chili's version has 787 calories per serving. By using diet margarine instead of oil, using low-fat cheese, and making the portions slightly smaller, you save 386 calories per serving.

CHILI'S
Chocolate Chip Paradise Pie

Crust

3 tablespoons diet margarine

⅓ cup graham cracker crumbs

3 packets Sweet'n Low (or your favorite reduced-calorie sugar substitute for cooking)

⅓ cup chocolate chips

Filling

½ cup all-purpose flour

4 packets Sweet'n Low (or your favorite reduced-calorie sugar substitute for cooking)

¾ teaspoon baking powder

⅓ cup skim milk

1 tablespoon diet margarine, melted

1 teaspoon vanilla extract

⅓ cup semisweet chocolate chips

¼ cup shredded coconut

¼ cup crushed walnuts

To Serve

¼ cup hot fudge sauce

¼ cup caramel sauce

¼ cup Cool Whip Lite topping

1. Preheat the oven to 350°F.

2. To make the crust, melt the margarine and combine with the graham cracker crumbs and sweetener.

3. Press into the bottom of a 1-quart baking dish. Top evenly with the chocolate chips.

4. Bake for 5 minutes, or until the chocolate is melted. Spread the melted chips out evenly over the crust.

5. To make the filling, combine the dry ingredients in a large mixing bowl.

6. Add the milk, margarine, and vanilla extract and stir until smooth. Stir in the chocolate chips, coconut, and walnuts. Pour into the crust.

7. Bake, uncovered, for 35 to 40 minutes, until a toothpick comes out clean.

8. Serve warm with 1 tablespoon each of fudge sauce, caramel sauce, and Cool Whip Lite.

Serves 4

Calories: 428
Fat: 21.15 grams
Protein: 5.80 grams
Carbohydrates: 59.11 grams
Dietary Fiber: 4.25 grams

The original Chili's version has 1,250 calories per serving. By using diet margarine and artificial sweetener, and Cool Whip Lite instead of ice cream as a topping, you save 822 calories per serving. If you eliminate the hot fudge and caramel toppings, you decrease the per-serving calories by an additional 100 calories.

CHILI'S
Margarita Grilled Chicken

⅔ cup lemon juice
⅓ cup lime juice
¼ cup tequila

1 tablespoon minced garlic
4 boneless, skinless chicken breasts
Salt and pepper

1. Combine the juices, tequila, and garlic in a dish with the chicken breasts and let marinate for 2 hours in the refrigerator. When ready to prepare, drain and season with salt and pepper.

2. Preheat the grill to medium-high heat.

3. Spray the grill with cooking spray and cook the chicken breasts until cooked through, 6 to 8 minutes on each side.

Serves 4

NUTRITIONAL INFORMATION (PER SERVING)

Calories: 305
Fat: 6.22 grams
Protein: 50.3 grams
Carbohydrates: 6.21 grams
Dietary Fiber: 0.24 grams

The original Chili's version has 600 calories per serving. By making your own margarita mix, using fresh lemon and lime juices, and not coating the chicken with oil, you save 295 calories per serving.

CHILI'S
Southwestern Chicken Chili

2 tablespoons diet margarine
½ cup diced onion
1⅓ cups diced green bell peppers
2 tablespoons diced jalapeño pepper
3 tablespoons minced garlic
4½ cups water
3 tablespoons chicken bouillon powder
2 teaspoons lime juice
2 packets Sweet'n Low (or your favorite reduced-calorie sugar substitute for cooking)
3 tablespoons cornstarch
3 tablespoons ground cumin
2½ tablespoons chili powder

4 teaspoons paprika
4 teaspoons dried basil
2 teaspoons minced fresh cilantro
1½ teaspoons cayenne pepper
½ teaspoon ground oregano
½ cup canned crushed tomatillos
One 4-ounce can diced green chiles, drained
Two 15-ounce cans pinto beans, rinsed and drained
One 15-ounce can red kidney beans, rinsed and drained
2 pounds cooked chicken breast, diced
Shredded low-fat Cheddar cheese, for garnish

1. In a 5-quart (or larger) pot, melt the margarine over medium heat. Add the onion and sauté along with the bell peppers, jalapeño pepper, and garlic. Cook until the vegetables are tender.

2. In a large bowl, combine the water, chicken bouillon powder, lime juice, sweetener, cornstarch, cumin, chili powder, paprika, basil, cilantro, cayenne pepper, and oregano. Add this to the vegetable mixture.

3. Add the tomatillos and diced green chiles to the pot; bring to a boil. Add the pinto beans and kidney beans and the chicken; simmer for 10 minutes.

4. Serve topped with cheese.

Serves 4

Calories: 595
Fat: 11.28 grams
Protein: 70.89 grams
Carbohydrates: 60.44 grams
Dietary Fiber: 14.25 grams

The original Chili's version has 790 calories per serving, with toppings of cheese, sour cream, and tortilla chips. By using diet margarine and artificial sweetener and a little less chicken, replacing the navy beans with pinto beans, and using only low-fat cheese on top, you save 195 calories per serving.

CRACKER BARREL
Baked Macaroni and Cheese

2 tablespoons diet margarine
2 tablespoons all-purpose flour
I teaspoon salt
I teaspoon dry mustard
2½ cups skim milk
2 cups shredded low-fat Cheddar
cheese

8 ounces whole wheat elbow
macaroni
I slice Sara Lee diet wheat bread
I teaspoon paprika

1. Preheat the oven to 375°F. Spray a 2-quart casserole with cooking spray; set aside.

2. In a medium saucepan, melt the margarine. While whisking, add the flour, salt, and dry mustard to the margarine. Add the milk and whisk constantly until the sauce thickens a little. Do not boil the milk. Add 1½ cups of the cheese and continue to cook until melted, stirring constantly. Remove from the heat.

3. Meanwhile, cook the macaroni as directed on the package; drain well, but do not rinse.

4. Toss the macaroni with the cheese sauce, coating well; transfer to the prepared casserole dish and top with the remaining ½ cup cheese.

5. Toast the slice of bread until it is lightly browned and thoroughly dry. Crumble into bread crumbs. Toss the crumbs with the paprika, then sprinkle over the top of the casserole.

6. Bake for 20 to 25 minutes, until heated through, bubbly, and nicely browned.

Serves 4

Calories: 380
Fat: 8.62 grams
Protein: 27.63 grams
Carbohydrates: 51.37 grams
Dietary Fiber: 2.21 grams

The original Cracker Barrel version has 437 calories per serving. By using diet margarine and diet bread, skim milk, low-fat cheese, and whole wheat macaroni, you save 57 calories per serving.

CRACKER BARREL
Banana Pudding

1 cup sugar
4 packets Sweet'n Low (or your
    favorite reduced-calorie sugar
    substitute for cooking)
½ cup plus 2 tablespoons all-
    purpose flour
½ teaspoon salt
4 cups skim milk
4 egg yolks, beaten

4 tablespoons (¼ cup) diet
    margarine
2 teaspoons vanilla extract
12 ounces sugar-free vanilla
    wafers
6 bananas, sliced about ⅓ inch
    thick
One 16-ounce container Cool
    Whip Lite topping

1. In a large saucepan over medium-low heat, combine the sugar, sweetener, flour, salt, and milk. Stir until completely blended.

2. When the mixture begins to boil, cook for 2 minutes, stirring constantly as it begins to thicken.

3. Remove from the heat and add ½ cup of the hot mixture to the beaten egg yolks and stir quickly until blended.

4. Place the pudding mixture back on the stove top over medium heat and add the egg yolk mixture; continue to cook, stirring, for 3 minutes.

5. After 3 minutes, turn the heat off, add the margarine and vanilla extract, and beat with a whisk until blended.

6. Remove from the stove top and let cool for about 10 minutes.

7. Spray a 13 by 9-inch baking pan with cooking spray and arrange the vanilla wafers to cover the bottom and sides of the pan.

8. Cover the wafers with the banana slices. Pour the pudding into the pan, covering the bananas and wafers.

9. Allow the banana pudding to cool in the refrigerator. When the pudding has set, cover with the Cool Whip Lite.

Serves 6

Calories: 585
Fat: 18.67 grams
Protein: 14.85 grams
Carbohydrates: 120.36 grams
Dietary Fiber: 1.48 grams

The original Cracker Barrel version has 895 calories per serving. By using artificial sweetener for part of the sugar, skim milk, diet margarine, and sugar-free vanilla wafers, you save 310 calories per serving.

CRACKER BARREL
Cherry-Chocolate Cobbler

1½ cups all-purpose flour
¼ cup sugar
6 packets Sweet'n Low (or your favorite reduced-calorie sugar substitute for cooking)
2 teaspoons baking powder
½ teaspoon salt
4 tablespoons (¼ cup) diet margarine, cut into small pieces

One 6-ounce package semisweet chocolate chips
¼ cup skim milk
1 egg
One 21-ounce can low-sugar cherry pie filling
¼ cup finely chopped pecans

1. Preheat the oven to 350°F.

2. In a large bowl, combine the flour, sugar, sweetener, baking powder, salt, and margarine; cut with a pastry blender until the crumbs are the size of large peas.

3. Using a double boiler, melt the semisweet chocolate chips.

4. Remove from the heat and let cool slightly at room temperature (about 5 minutes).

5. Add the milk and egg to the melted chocolate and mix well.

6. Blend the chocolate mixture into the flour mixture.

7. Spread the cherry pie filling in the bottom of a 2-quart casserole. Drop the chocolate batter randomly over the cherries. Sprinkle with the nuts.

8. Bake for 40 to 45 minutes, until the top is golden brown. Serve hot.

Serves 6

Calories: 348
Fat: 14.79 grams
Protein: 5.74 grams
Carbohydrates: 47.55 grams
Dietary Fiber: 3.25 grams

The original Cracker Barrel version has 510 calories per serving. By using artificial sweetener for part of the sugar, diet margarine, skim milk, and low-sugar cherry pie filling, you save 162 calories per serving.

CRACKER BARREL
Chicken Salad

2 pounds boneless, skinless chicken breasts
2 ribs celery, cut into chunks
2 chicken bouillon cubes
2 tablespoons dill pickle relish
2 tablespoons finely diced onion
1/4 cup finely minced celery
2/3 cup fat-free mayonnaise

1/3 cup fat-free sour cream
2 tablespoons Miracle Whip Light salad dressing
Torn lettuce leaves
8 ounces low-fat Cheddar cheese, cut into wedges
2 tomatoes, quartered

1. Place the chicken breasts in a saucepan; add the celery chunks and bouillon cubes. Add cold water to cover and cook the chicken until tender. Remove the chicken from the broth and refrigerate until very cold. (This is a great make-ahead dish or even a good way to use leftover chicken.) Freeze the broth for use on another day.

2. Dice the cold chicken into bite-sized pieces. Transfer the chicken to a large bowl and add the relish, onion, and celery.

3. In a small bowl, combine the mayonnaise, sour cream, and salad dressing; blend well. Pour over the chicken mixture and mix well.

4. To serve, use an ice cream scoop and place a scoop of chicken salad on torn lettuce leaves. Add a 1-ounce wedge of cheese and a tomato quarter to each plate. Serve immediately.

Serves 8

NUTRITIONAL INFORMATION (PER SERVING)

Calories:	215
Fat:	6.23 grams
Protein:	7.20 grams
Carbohydrates:	6.78 grams
Dietary Fiber:	0.56 gram

The original Cracker Barrel version has 620 calories per serving. By using fat-free mayonnaise, fat-free sour cream, light salad dressing, and low-fat cheese and slightly decreasing the serving size (4 ounces of chicken with all the extras is plenty for one person), you save 405 calories per serving. If you eliminate the cheese from the dish, you save another 50 calories per serving.

DANIEL

Short Ribs Braised in Red Wine

2 bottles dry red wine
8 short ribs, trimmed of excess fat
Salt and coarsely ground pepper
1 tablespoon diet margarine
8 large shallots, split in half
2 medium carrots, cut into 1-inch lengths
2 ribs celery, peeled and cut into 1-inch lengths

1 medium leek, roughly chopped
10 cloves garlic, peeled
6 sprigs fresh Italian parsley
2 bay leaves
2 sprigs fresh thyme
2 tablespoons tomato paste
8 cups beef broth

1. Pour the wine into a large saucepan over medium heat. When the wine is hot, carefully set it aflame. Let the flames die out, then increase the heat so that the wine boils. Allow it to boil until it cooks down by half. Remove from the heat.

2. Season the ribs with salt and pepper.

3. Preheat the oven to 350°F.

4. Melt the margarine in a large ovenproof pot. Sear the ribs for about 4 minutes on each side in the margarine. Transfer the ribs to a plate and repeat until all the ribs are seared.

5. Add the shallots, carrots, celery, leek, garlic, parsley, bay leaves, and thyme to the pot. Lightly brown the vegetables for 5 to 7 minutes. Stir in the tomato paste and cook for 1 minute.

6. Add the wine, ribs, and beef broth to the pot. Bring to a boil, cover tightly, and place in the oven to braise for 2½ hours. Every 30 minutes, skim and discard any fat on the surface.

7. Transfer the ribs to a platter.

8. Boil the liquid in the pot until it has reduced to 4 cups. Season with salt and pepper as needed and pass through a fine-mesh strainer. Discard any solids.

9. Serve 1 rib on each plate with sauce spooned over the top.

Serves 8

Recipe adapted from "Chef Daniel Boulud's Short Ribs Braised in Red Wine with Celery Duo," Parade, *December 2000.*

NUTRITIONAL INFORMATION (PER SERVING)

Calories:	1,190
Fat:	76.51 grams
Protein:	40.92 grams
Carbohydrates:	8.82 grams
Dietary Fiber:	1.20 grams

The original Daniel version has 1,320 calories per serving. By searing the ribs in diet margarine rather than oil and decreasing the amount of liquid, you save 130 calories per serving.

DAVE AND BUSTER'S
Blackened Chicken Pasta

Cajun Blackening Spice
¼ cup paprika
3 tablespoons garlic powder
2 tablespoons celery salt
1 tablespoon onion powder
1 tablespoon ground cumin
1 teaspoon cayenne pepper
1 teaspoon dried thyme
1 teaspoon chili powder

Chicken and Pasta Sauce
1 tablespoon diet margarine
6 ounces boneless, skinless chicken
breast, cut into bite-sized pieces

1 cup sliced mushrooms
2 teaspoons poultry seasoning
1 teaspoon minced garlic
⅓ cup diced Roma tomatoes
3 ounces fat-free cream cheese,
softened
1 cup skim milk
1 tablespoon grated Parmesan
cheese

To Serve
6 ounces linguine, cooked until al
dente
1 teaspoon chopped fresh parsley

1. Make the Cajun blackening spice ahead of time by combining all the ingredients. Store in a tightly covered container until ready to use.

2. Melt the margarine in a skillet and sauté the chicken and mushrooms. Sprinkle with the poultry seasoning and cook the chicken all the way through. Add the garlic and diced tomatoes and sauté for another minute.

3. Lower the heat and add 2 teaspoons of the Cajun blackening spice, the cream cheese, and the skim milk. Stir well to combine the ingredients, then remove from the heat and add the Parmesan cheese.

4. Portion the cooked linguine onto 2 warmed serving plates by using tongs and swirling and mounding the pasta onto each plate. Top with the chicken and sauce. Sprinkle with the chopped parsley.

Serves 2

Calories: 625
Fat: 12.85 grams
Protein: 40.54 grams
Carbohydrates: 90.50 grams
Dietary Fiber: 20.55 grams

The original Dave and Buster's version has 1,279 calories per serving. By using diet margarine, skim milk, and fat-free cream cheese instead of oil, Alfredo sauce, and heavy cream, and cutting the amount of pasta back slightly for each serving, you more than cut the calories in half and save 654 calories per serving.

DAVE AND BUSTER'S
Cajun Shrimp Alfredo

8 ounces fresh linguine or
fettuccine
10 ounces large shrimp, peeled and
deveined
3 tablespoons Cajun seasoning
3 tablespoons diet margarine
1½ cups chopped mushrooms
2 teaspoons minced garlic

¾ cup diced tomatoes
½ cup skim milk
3 ounces low-fat cream cheese,
softened
½ cup grated low-fat Parmesan
cheese
1 egg yolk
½ cup chopped green onions

1. Bring a large pot of salted water to a boil; add the pasta and cook until al dente. Drain, but do not rinse.

2. Meanwhile, toss the shrimp in 1 tablespoon of the Cajun seasoning.

3. In a heavy skillet, melt the margarine. Add the seasoned shrimp and sauté for about 1 minute, turning several times during the cooking process.

4. Add the mushrooms and continue to cook for several minutes. Add the garlic and tomatoes, continue stirring, and sauté for a few seconds.

5. Add the milk, cream cheese, and remaining 2 tablespoons Cajun seasoning; bring to a simmer, but do not boil.

6. Add the Parmesan cheese, egg yolk, and green onions; stir over medium heat until the sauce thickens, but do not boil. (Control your heat source: Too high a heat will cause the egg yolk to curdle and look scrambled.)

7. Place the drained pasta in a serving bowl and pour the sauce over the top. Toss lightly to coat.

Serves 4

Calories: 420
Fat: 10 grams
Protein: 28.36 grams
Carbohydrates: 54.82 grams
Dietary Fiber: 7.04 grams

The original Dave and Buster's version has 725 calories per serving. By using diet margarine, skim milk, and low-fat cheeses, you save 305 calories per serving.

DAVE AND BUSTER'S
Cheddar Mashed Potatoes

Garlic Butter

1 teaspoon minced garlic

6 tablespoons diet margarine, softened

1 teaspoon chopped fresh parsley

Potatoes

2 pounds red potatoes, scrubbed and cut into 1-inch chunks

⅓ cup skim milk

4 ounces low-fat white Cheddar cheese, shredded

Salt and pepper

1. Make the garlic butter by lightly sautéing the garlic in 1 tablespoon of the margarine until soft but not browned. Add the remaining 5 tablespoons margarine and the parsley. Gently whisk everything together and pour into a covered container. Refrigerate until ready to use.

2. Cook the potatoes in boiling salted water until they are soft, 5 to 10 minutes, then drain well. Place them in a warmed serving bowl and add the milk, cheese, and ¼ cup of the garlic butter. Mash with a fork or beat very lightly with a hand mixer. Season with salt and pepper.

Serves 4

NUTRITIONAL INFORMATION (PER SERVING)

Calories: 325

Fat: 13.40 grams

Protein: 12.92 grams

Carbohydrates: 48.08 grams

Dietary Fiber: 4.10 grams

The original Dave and Buster's version has 377 calories per serving. By using diet margarine, skim milk, and low-fat cheese, you save 52 calories per serving.

DAVE AND BUSTER'S
Steak Fajita Salad

Dressing

One 1-ounce package buttermilk
    ranch salad dressing mix
½ cup fat-free mayonnaise
½ cup fat-free sour cream
¼ cup low-fat buttermilk
1 cup chopped fresh cilantro
2 cloves garlic, minced
¼ teaspoon cayenne pepper

Salad

6 ounces flank or skirt steak
One 1.12-ounce package fajita
    seasoning mix
Two 6-inch flour tortillas
6 ounces romaine hearts, chopped
½ cup grated low-fat Cheddar
    cheese
¼ cup diced onion

1. Combine all the dressing ingredients in a blender and process until smooth. Refrigerate in a covered container until ready to use.

2. Coat the steak with the fajita seasoning mix on both sides. Allow to marinate in the refrigerator for at least 30 minutes.

3. Preheat the grill to medium heat or preheat the broiler.

4. Grill the steak to the desired doneness. Allow to cool for about 10 minutes, then cut the steak against the grain into thin strips.

5. Place the flour tortillas on the hot grill, lightly browning both sides. Allow the tortillas to cool and then break into bite-sized pieces.

6. Toss the romaine with the cheese and onion and divide between two serving plates.

7. Spoon the dressing onto the salad and top with the strips of steak and the tortilla pieces.

Serves 2

Calories: 489
Fat: 22.11 grams
Protein: 29.58 grams
Carbohydrates: 32.94 grams
Dietary Fiber: 4.05 grams

The original Dave and Buster's version has 1,408 calories per serving. By using fat-free mayonnaise and sour cream, using low-fat cheese, cutting the amount of steak per serving slightly, controlling extra toppings, and serving with tortilla pieces rather than in a large tortilla bowl, you save 919 calories per serving.

FAMOUS DAVE'S
Shakin' the Shack Potato Salad

3 pounds russet potatoes, scrubbed
1 cup fat-free mayonnaise
1/2 cup fat-free sour cream
1 tablespoon yellow mustard
1 tablespoon white vinegar
1 teaspoon salt
1 packet Sweet'n Low (or your favorite reduced-calorie sugar substitute for cooking)
1/2 teaspoon pepper
1/2 cup minced celery
1/2 cup minced red onion
1/2 cup minced green bell pepper
2 tablespoons minced pimiento
1 tablespoon minced jalapeño pepper
3 hard-boiled eggs, minced
1/4 cup pickle relish
Paprika, for garnish

1. Put the potatoes in a pot and cover with water. Boil until they are tender and cooked through but not mushy. Drain and refrigerate until cold.

2. In a large bowl, combine the mayonnaise, sour cream, mustard, vinegar, salt, sweetener, and pepper and refrigerate until ready to use.

3. Peel the skins from the cold potatoes and coarsely chop the potatoes.

4. Combine the celery, red onion, bell pepper, pimiento, and jalapeño. Add to the mayonnaise mixture, then fold in the potatoes, eggs, and relish.

5. Sprinkle the top with a light dusting of paprika.

Serves 8

NUTRITIONAL INFORMATION (PER SERVING)

Calories: 216
Fat: 3.13 grams
Protein: 6.01 grams
Carbohydrates: 42.63 grams
Dietary Fiber: 4.23 grams

The original Famous Dave's version has 260 calories per serving. By using fat-free mayonnaise and sour cream and using fewer eggs, you save 44 calories per serving.

GOLDEN CORRAL
Banana Pudding

One 14-ounce can fat-free
sweetened condensed milk
1½ cups cold skim milk
One 3½-ounce package sugar-free
vanilla instant pudding

2 cups Cool Whip Lite topping,
thawed
3 bananas, sliced
6 ounces vanilla wafers, plus more
for garnish

1. In a large bowl, mix the sweetened condensed milk with the skim milk. Add the pudding mix and beat well. Chill in the refrigerator for 5 minutes.

2. Fold in the thawed Cool Whip.

3. Spread 1 cup of the pudding on the bottom of a large serving dish. Top with one-third of the bananas, one-third of the wafers, and one-third of the pudding. Repeat the layering twice, ending with the pudding. Garnish with a few crushed vanilla wafers on top. Chill thoroughly and keep refrigerated until ready to serve.

Makes twelve ½-cup servings

Note: The pudding part of this recipe can be made a day in advance. Just assemble with the bananas and cookies shortly before serving. Also, the bananas can be stirred into the pudding, if you prefer, instead of layered on top of the pudding.

NUTRITIONAL INFORMATION (PER SERVING)

Calories: 225
Fat: 3.96 grams
Protein: 12.36 grams
Carbohydrates: 44.69 grams
Dietary Fiber: 1.07 grams

The original Golden Corral version has 250 calories per ½-cup serving. By using fat-free milks, sugar-free pudding, and Cool Whip Lite and cutting the amount of cookies down, you save 25 calories per serving.

GOLDEN CORRAL
Bourbon Street Chicken

½ cup soy sauce
4 packets Sweet'n Low (or your favorite reduced-calorie sugar substitute for cooking)
½ teaspoon garlic powder
1 teaspoon ground ginger
2 tablespoons onion flakes
¼ cup bourbon
¼ cup plus 2 tablespoons chicken broth
1 pound boneless, skinless chicken thighs, cut into bite-sized pieces

1. Whisk together the soy sauce, sweetener, garlic powder, ginger, onion flakes, bourbon, and the ¼ cup chicken broth. Pour over the chicken pieces in a bowl and marinate in the refrigerator for 4 hours, stirring occasionally.

2. Preheat the oven to 350°F.

3. After the chicken has marinated, transfer it to a metal baking pan or an iron skillet and arrange the pieces in a single layer. Pour any marinade left in the bowl over the chicken pieces and bake for 1 hour, stirring and basting with the marinade about every 10 minutes.

4. When the chicken is cooked through, transfer it to a plate and keep it warm. Place the baking pan or skillet over a stovetop burner and deglaze the pan over medium heat using the 2 tablespoons chicken broth.

5. Add the chicken to the baking pan or skillet and simmer for 5 minutes. Serve warm.

Serves 4

Calories: 190
Fat: 4.88 grams
Protein: 28.42 grams
Carbohydrates: 1.65 grams
Dietary Fiber: 0.25 gram

The original Golden Corral version has 215 calories per serving. By using artificial sweetener and substituting chicken broth for some of the bourbon and the white wine, you save 25 calories per serving.

GOLDEN CORRAL
Rolls

1 envelope (2¼ teaspoons) active dry yeast

¼ cup warm water (105° to 115°F)

1 teaspoon sugar

3 packets Sweet'n Low (or your favorite reduced-calorie sugar substitute for cooking)

4 tablespoons (¼ cup) diet margarine

1 teaspoon salt

1 cup hot skim milk

1 egg, beaten

4½ cups all-purpose flour, sifted

1. In a large bowl, sprinkle the yeast over the warm water and let it proof, about 5 minutes.

2. In another bowl, combine the sugar, sweetener, 3 tablespoons of the margarine, the salt, and hot milk. Stir with a wooden spoon until the margarine is melted and the sugar and sweetener are dissolved. Let the mixture cool to 105° to 115°F, then add it to the proofed yeast mixture along with the beaten egg.

3. Add the flour 1 cup at a time, mixing well after each addition. After the fourth cup, form the dough into a soft ball. Sprinkle some of the remaining ½ cup flour onto a work surface and knead the dough for about 5 minutes, gradually working in all the remaining flour. Spray the inside of a bowl with cooking spray and put the dough in it. Spray the top of the dough lightly with cooking spray. Cover the dough with a damp towel and set the bowl in a warm area free from drafts.

4. When the dough has doubled in size, 1 to 1½ hours, punch it down, turn it out onto a lightly floured work surface, and knead for 4 to 5 minutes. Spray an 18 by 13-inch baking sheet with cooking spray and set aside.

5. Pinch off small chunks of dough and shape them into balls 1½ to 1¾ inches across until you have 24 rolls. Place the rolls on the prepared baking sheet so they do not touch one another. Cover with a damp towel and let rise in a warm, draft-free place until doubled in size, 30 to 40 minutes.

6. Preheat the oven to 375°F.

7. Melt the remaining 1 tablespoon margarine. Using a pastry brush, brush the tops of the risen rolls with the melted margarine and bake for 18 to 20 minutes, until they are browned on top.

Makes 24 rolls

NUTRITIONAL INFORMATION (PER SERVING)

Calories:	101
Fat:	1.62 grams
Protein:	3.18 grams
Carbohydrates:	18.75 grams
Dietary Fiber:	0.71 gram

The original Golden Corral version has 120 calories per roll. By using artificial sweetener for some of the sugar and using diet margarine, you save 19 calories per roll.

GOLDEN CORRAL
Seafood Salad

8 ounces imitation crabmeat, shredded
1 cup small shrimp, peeled, deveined, and cooked
1 large green bell pepper, minced
1 medium onion, minced
½ cup fat-free ranch salad dressing
¼ cup fat-free mayonnaise
Lettuce leaves

1. Gently mix all the ingredients together except the lettuce leaves, and refrigerate for about 1 hour.

2. When you are ready to serve, line six salad plates with lettuce leaves and place about ½ cup of the salad on top of each plate.

Serves 6

NUTRITIONAL INFORMATION (PER SERVING)
Calories: 90
Fat: 1.47 grams
Protein: 10.04 grams
Carbohydrates: 9.24 grams
Dietary Fiber: 0.57 gram

The original Golden Corral version has 140 calories per serving. By using fat-free ranch dressing and fat-free mayonnaise, you save 50 calories per serving.

HARD ROCK CAFE
Baked Potato Soup

8 slices turkey bacon
1 cup diced yellow onions
1 tablespoon diet margarine
⅓ cup all-purpose flour
½ cup potato flakes
6 cups hot chicken broth
4 cups diced peeled baked potatoes
2 cups skim milk
¼ cup fat-free sour cream
¼ cup chopped fresh parsley, plus more for garnish

1½ teaspoons granulated garlic
1½ teaspoons dried basil
1½ teaspoons salt
1½ teaspoons Tabasco sauce
1½ teaspoons coarsely ground pepper
1 cup grated low-fat Cheddar cheese
¼ cup diced green onions, plus more for garnish

1. Fry the bacon until crisp. Drain on paper towels and crumble.

2. Cook the yellow onions in the margarine over medium-high heat until soft, about 3 minutes.

3. Add the flour, whisking to prevent lumps. Cook for 4 minutes.

4. Whisk in the potato flakes.

5. Slowly add the chicken broth, whisking to prevent lumps, and cook until the liquid thickens.

6. Reduce the heat to a simmer and add the potatoes, milk, sour cream, crumbled bacon, parsley, garlic, basil, salt, Tabasco sauce, and pepper. Simmer for 10 minutes, but do not boil.

7. Add the grated cheese and green onions. Heat until the cheese melts.

8. Serve, garnished with additional chopped parsley or diced green onions.

Serves 6

Calories:	285
Fat:	4.19 grams
Protein:	16.52 grams
Carbohydrates:	45.43 grams
Dietary Fiber:	2.48 grams

The original Hard Rock Cafe version has 695 calories per serving. By using turkey bacon, skim milk and fat-free sour cream instead of heavy cream, potato flakes as a substitute for some of the flour for thickening, and low-fat Cheddar cheese, and eliminating the extra bacon and cheese on top, you save 410 calories per serving.

HARD ROCK CAFE
Blackened Chicken Penne Pasta

Marinade
2 tablespoons lemon juice
2 tablespoons soy sauce
1 tablespoon lime juice
1 tablespoon Worcestershire sauce

8 ounces boneless, skinless chicken breasts

Cajun Chicken Seasoning Mix
1 tablespoon kosher salt
1 tablespoon garlic pepper
1 tablespoon white pepper
1/2 teaspoon cayenne pepper
1/2 teaspoon onion powder

1 tablespoon diet margarine, melted
One 3-ounce package fat-free cream cheese, softened
2 tablespoons grated fat-free Parmesan cheese
1/2 teaspoon dried basil
1/2 teaspoon dried oregano
1/2 teaspoon salt
1/2 teaspoon black pepper
8 ounces penne pasta, cooked until al dente
3/4 cup baby spinach leaves
1/4 cup diced tomatoes
1 tablespoon chopped fresh parsley

1. Combine all the marinade ingredients with 1 cup water.

2. Marinate the chicken breasts in the refrigerator for at least 4 hours or up to overnight.

3. Mix the Cajun seasoning ingredients together in a small bowl.

4. Preheat the grill to medium heat or preheat the broiler.

5. Remove the chicken from the marinade and season both sides with the Cajun seasoning. Discard the marinade. Grill the chicken until cooked through and no longer pink in the middle, turning once. When cool enough to handle, cut into 5 or 6 slices.

6. In a medium bowl, mix the melted margarine, the cream cheese, 1 tablespoon of the Parmesan cheese, the basil, oregano, salt, and black pepper until smooth. Pour the cream cheese mixture over the penne pasta in the saucepan you cooked the pasta in.

7. Stir in the spinach and tomatoes and heat thoroughly.

8. Transfer the pasta to a serving bowl and add the sliced chicken. Sprinkle with the remaining 1 tablespoon Parmesan cheese and garnish with the chopped parsley.

Serves 2

NUTRITIONAL INFORMATION (PER SERVING)

Calories:	575
Fat:	10.21 grams
Protein:	46 grams
Carbohydrates:	97.03 grams
Dietary Fiber:	13.60 grams

The original Hard Rock Cafe version has 875 calories per serving. By using diet margarine and fat-free cheeses and eliminating the rich Alfredo sauce and accompanying garlic toast, you save 300 calories per serving.

HARD ROCK CAFE
Chili

2 tablespoons diet margarine
2½ pounds extra-lean beef (95% lean), coarsely ground for chili
1 large onion, chopped
3 large cloves garlic, crushed
One 6-ounce can tomato sauce
2 tablespoons Worcestershire sauce
2 tablespoons chili powder
4 packets Sweet'n Low (or your favorite reduced-calorie sugar substitute for cooking)
1 tablespoon soy sauce
2 teaspoons celery salt

1 teaspoon ground cumin
1 teaspoon black pepper
1 teaspoon seasoned salt
1 teaspoon onion flakes
1 teaspoon granulated garlic
½ teaspoon cayenne pepper
One 15-ounce can diced tomatoes, with juice
¾ cup kidney beans, drained and rinsed
One 4-ounce jar pimientos, coarsely chopped, with liquid
1 medium green bell pepper, chopped
¼ cup diced celery

1. Melt the margarine in a large saucepan or a Dutch oven and sauté the ground beef until browned. Drain the fat and add the onion and garlic, and sauté until they are soft. Set aside.

2. Separately, mix together the tomato sauce, Worcestershire sauce, chili powder, sweetener, soy sauce, celery salt, cumin, black pepper, seasoned salt, onion flakes, granulated garlic, and cayenne pepper. Stir until the spices are all well blended.

3. Add the tomato sauce mixture to the meat mixture and simmer for 5 minutes. Stir in the canned diced tomatoes with their juice and the drained kidney beans. Reduce the heat to low and cook, covered, for about 15 minutes, stirring occasionally. Add the pimientos with their liquid, the bell pepper, and the celery, and simmer, uncovered, for about 5 minutes more. Serve while hot.

Serves 6

Calories: 290
Fat: 10.80 grams
Protein: 40.99 grams
Carbohydrates: 4.01 grams
Dietary Fiber: 0.97 gram

The original Hard Rock Cafe version has 665 calories per serving, including the crackers it is served with. By using diet margarine, extra-lean beef, and tomato sauce instead of tomato paste and barbecue sauce, you save 375 calories per serving. (That is, if you refrain from serving crackers with your chili. But you can add the saltine crackers for 12 calories per cracker.)

HARD ROCK CAFE
Love Me Tenders with Sauce

Sauce
1 cup yellow mustard
¼ cup honey
3 packets Sweet'n Low (or your favorite reduced-calorie sugar substitute for cooking)
¼ cup low-fat mayonnaise

¼ cup egg substitute (such as Egg Beaters)
¼ cup skim milk
4 slices Sara Lee diet wheat bread
¼ teaspoon onion powder
¼ teaspoon garlic powder
Salt and pepper
2 pounds chicken tenderloins

1. Make the sauce: In a small bowl, combine the sauce ingredients and blend well; refrigerate, covered, until ready to serve.

2. Preheat the oven to 350°F.

3. In a medium bowl, combine the egg substitute and milk; mix well.

4. Toast the bread until it is thoroughly dried. Crumble the bread into bread crumbs. Add the onion powder, garlic powder, and salt and pepper to taste to the bread crumbs.

5. Dip the chicken strips in the egg mixture, coating evenly, then roll the chicken strips in the bread crumb mixture and press to coat.

6. Place the coated chicken strips on a baking sheet that has been sprayed with cooking spray. Bake for about 20 minutes, until the strips are cooked through.

7. Serve with the prepared sauce.

Serves 8

Calories: 215
Fat: 4.62 grams
Protein: 27.66 grams
Carbohydrates: 14.14 grams
Dietary Fiber: 0.98 gram

The original Hard Rock Cafe version has 440 calories per serving. By using egg substitute, skim milk, homemade bread crumbs, artificial sweetener, and low-fat mayonnaise, and baking instead of frying, you save 225 calories per serving.

HARD ROCK CAFE
Nice and Easy Chicken 'n' Cheesy

Two 6-ounce boneless, skinless chicken breasts, cut into ½-inch pieces
1 tablespoon diet margarine
½ habanero pepper, minced
2 large tomatoes, diced
1 small onion, chopped
1 teaspoon garlic powder
1 teaspoon onion powder

¼ cup chopped fresh cilantro
1 tablespoon apple cider vinegar
¼ cup chicken bouillon powder
½ teaspoon paprika
1 tablespoon ground cumin
1 teaspoon chili powder
½ teaspoon garlic salt
1 cup low-fat Cheddar cheese
1 lime, cut into quarters

1. Preheat the oven to 375°F.

2. Spray a baking sheet with cooking spray. Place the chicken in a single layer on the baking sheet and bake for about 20 minutes, until cooked through.

3. Melt the margarine in a large stockpot and sauté the habanero pepper. Add the tomatoes, onion, garlic powder, onion powder, cilantro, and vinegar. Cook for about 5 minutes, until the vegetables are soft.

4. Add 8 cups of warm water, the chicken bouillon powder, the spices, and the garlic salt to the pot. Simmer for about 15 minutes, until reduced by half. Taste and adjust the seasonings as needed.

5. Divide the cheese among four bowls. Add the cooked chicken pieces to the bowls. Ladle the broth over the top. Attach a lime quarter to the side of each bowl.

Serves 4

Calories: 195
Fat: 6.17 grams
Protein: 25.46 grams
Carbohydrates: 5.81 grams
Dietary Fiber: 1.58 grams

The original Hard Rock Cafe version has 395 calories per serving. By using diet margarine and low-fat cheese, and eliminating the tortilla strips and sour cream on top of the dish, you save 200 calories per serving.

HARD ROCK CAFE
Pulled Pork

4 cups apple cider vinegar
½ cup Tabasco sauce
¼ cup sugar
4 packets Sweet'n Low (or your favorite reduced-calorie sugar substitute for cooking)

4 cups hot water
2 pounds pork shoulder

1. Marinate the pork: In a large bowl, combine the apple cider vinegar, Tabasco sauce, sugar, sweetener, and hot water. Stir until the sugar is dissolved. Pour the marinade over the pork, cover, and refrigerate overnight.

2. Preheat the oven to 450°F.

3. Remove the pork from the marinade and place in a baking pan. Save the marinade. Roast the pork until browned, about 1 hour.

4. Reduce the oven temperature to 300°F, pour some of the reserved marinade over the pork, cover, and slow-roast for an additional 1½ hours, or until the meat pulls away from the bone easily.

5. Pull the pork apart into long shreds using two forks.

Serves 6

NUTRITIONAL INFORMATION (PER SERVING)

Calories:	426
Fat:	27.42 grams
Protein:	26.35 grams
Carbohydrates:	10.05 grams
Dietary Fiber:	0 grams

The original Hard Rock Cafe version has 637 calories per serving. Since there are so few ingredients in this recipe, you can substitute artificial sweetener for some of the sugar, but the best calorie-saver is serving smaller portions. With 2 pounds of pork shoulder, the portion sizes are still over 5 ounces and you save 211 calories per serving.

HARD ROCK CAFE
Shrimp Fajitas

1 pound medium shrimp, peeled and deveined
1 cup chopped fresh cilantro
2 cloves garlic, minced
⅓ cup lime juice
Four 6-inch flour tortillas

1 tablespoon diet margarine
2 large bell peppers (1 red, 1 green), thinly sliced
1 large onion, thinly sliced
½ cup fat-free sour cream

1. Preheat the oven to 350°F.

2. Stir together the shrimp, cilantro, garlic, and lime juice. Let stand at room temperature for 20 minutes.

3. Meanwhile, wrap the tortillas in foil and place in the oven until warm, about 7 or 8 minutes.

4. Melt the margarine in a large nonstick skillet over medium-high heat. Add the peppers and onion. Cook, stirring occasionally, until the vegetables are limp, about 10 minutes. Remove the vegetables from the pan and keep warm.

5. Add the shrimp mixture to the pan, increase the heat to high, and cook, stirring often, until the shrimp are opaque in the center, about 3 minutes. Return the vegetables to the pan, stirring to mix with the shrimp.

6. Spoon the shrimp mixture onto the warm tortillas, top with the sour cream, and roll up.

Serves 4

Calories: 156
Fat: 3.6 grams
Protein: 12.98 grams
Carbohydrates: 18.5 grams
Dietary Fiber: 2.2 grams

The original Hard Rock Cafe version has 280 calories per serving. By using smaller tortillas, substituting diet margarine for the oil, and using fat-free sour cream, you save 124 calories per serving.

HARDEE'S
Cinnamon "Flake" Biscuits

"Flake" Mixture
One 13-ounce box bran flakes
1 tablespoon ground cinnamon
1 tablespoon light brown sugar
3 packets Sweet'n Low (or your favorite reduced-calorie sugar substitute for cooking)
2 tablespoons diet margarine, melted

Biscuit Dough
2½ cups biscuit mix, plus more as needed
6 packets Sweet'n Low (or your favorite reduced-calorie sugar substitute for cooking)

½ cup dark raisins
⅓ cup buttermilk
½ cup tonic water
½ teaspoon vanilla extract

Icing
1 tablespoon diet margarine, melted
1 teaspoon vanilla extract
1 tablespoon fat-free sour cream
Pinch of salt
½ cup confectioners' sugar

1. Preheat the oven to 400°F. Spray two 8-inch round cake pans with cooking spray.

2. To make the "flake" mixture, empty the box of cereal into a blender. Add the cinnamon, brown sugar, and sweetener and pulse on high speed for about 3 seconds, until the mixture is crumbled but not powdered.

3. Empty into a small bowl. Stir in the melted margarine with a fork. Set aside.

4. To make the biscuit dough, in a 2-quart mixing bowl, stir the biscuit mix together with the sweetener and raisins.

5. Pour the buttermilk, tonic water, and vanilla extract into the dry mixture. Use a fork to mix until all of the liquid is absorbed, then knead in the bowl with your hands. (Add sprinkles of additional biscuit mix if needed to make the dough smooth and prevent it from sticking.)

6. Break the dough into 5 portions in the bowl. Sprinkle the "flake" mixture over the dough and then work it in until most of it is evenly distributed throughout the dough.

7. Divide the dough into 12 equal parts and shape each portion into a ½-inch-thick patty. Arrange the patties close together in the prepared cake pans. Bake for 25 minutes, or until golden.

8. While the biscuits are baking, make the icing: In a small bowl with an electric mixer on high speed, beat the melted margarine, vanilla extract, sour cream, salt, and confectioners' sugar until smooth.

9. When the biscuits are done, remove the pan to a wire rack and drizzle the biscuits with the icing.

Serves 12

NUTRITIONAL INFORMATION (PER SERVING)

Calories:	225
Fat:	6.72 grams
Protein:	4.47 grams
Carbohydrates:	47.32 grams
Dietary Fiber:	7.24 grams

The original Hardee's version has 300 calories per biscuit. By substituting artificial sweetener for some of the sugar and making the icing more of a drizzle than a thick coating, you save 75 calories per biscuit.

HARDEE'S
Peach Cobbler

Filling

¼ cup all-purpose flour

One 29-ounce can peach slices packed in water (not syrup), with liquid

4 packets Sweet'n Low (or your favorite reduced-calorie sugar substitute for cooking)

1 teaspoon ground cinnamon

2 tablespoons diet margarine

Crust

1 cup all-purpose flour

1 packet Sweet'n Low (or your favorite reduced-calorie sugar substitute for cooking)

4 tablespoons (¼ cup) diet margarine

2 to 3 tablespoons ice water

1 teaspoon ground cinnamon

1. Preheat the oven to 375°F.

2. To make the filling, place the flour in a medium bowl and add a little of the liquid from the peaches. Using a whisk, incorporate the flour into the liquid. When the mixture is smooth, add the peaches and the rest of the liquid and stir well. Add the sweetener and cinnamon and stir. Pour the mixture into an 8 by 8-inch pan. Dot the peaches with the margarine, so the melted margarine will spread out over the filling as it bakes.

3. To make the crust, place the flour in a medium bowl. Add the sweetener. Using a fork or pastry cutter, add the margarine to the flour. Incorporate the margarine into the flour until the mixture is clumpy. Gradually add the ice water until the dough can be formed into a ball. Roll the dough on a floured cutting board to about ¼ inch thick and cut the dough into strips. Place the strips across the top of the peach filling. (You can do a basket weave or make a design, depending on how much time you want to spend making the top look fancy.)

4. Sprinkle the cinnamon on top of the crust.

5. Bake for 20 to 25 minutes, until the crust is lightly browned.

Serves 4

Calories: 240
Fat: 10.89 grams
Protein: 4.54 grams
Carbohydrates: 37.54 grams
Dietary Fiber: 2.63 grams

The original Hardee's version has 285 calories per serving. By using peaches packed in water instead of peach pie filling and making your own crust, you save 45 calories per serving.

HOUSTON'S
Spinach and Artichoke Dip

Two 10-ounce boxes frozen spinach, thawed
1 tablespoon minced garlic
2 tablespoons minced onion
4 tablespoons (¼ cup) diet margarine
¼ cup all-purpose flour
2 cups skim milk
¼ cup chicken broth
2 teaspoons lemon juice
½ teaspoon Tabasco sauce
½ teaspoon salt
⅔ cup grated low-fat Romano cheese
¼ cup fat-free sour cream
One 12-ounce jar artichoke hearts, drained and coarsely chopped
½ cup shredded low-fat white Cheddar cheese

1. Drain the spinach and squeeze through a cheesecloth to remove as much liquid as possible; mince and set aside.

2. In a heavy saucepan over medium heat, cook the garlic and onion in the margarine, stirring, for 3 to 5 minutes, until golden.

3. Stir in the flour and cook, stirring, for 1 minute.

4. Stir in the milk and broth and cook until boiling.

5. Once boiling, stir in the lemon juice, Tabasco sauce, salt, and Romano cheese; stir until the cheese has melted.

6. Remove from the heat and let cool for 5 minutes.

7. Stir in the sour cream, then fold in the spinach and artichoke hearts.

8. Transfer to a microwave-safe serving bowl and sprinkle the Cheddar cheese evenly over the top.

9. Microwave to melt the Cheddar cheese, and serve.

Serves 12

Calories: 85
Fat: 3.34 grams
Protein: 6.49 grams
Carbohydrates: 8.44 grams
Dietary Fiber: 2.69 grams

The original Houston's version has 262 calories per serving. By using diet margarine, skim milk, low-fat cheeses, and fat-free sour cream, you save 177 calories per serving.

IHOP

Colorado Omelet

1 tablespoon diet margarine	⅓ cup sliced cooked small
¼ cup diced yellow onion	breakfast turkey sausage links
¼ cup diced green bell pepper	¼ cup crumbled cooked turkey
¼ cup diced cooked turkey ham	bacon
4 eggs, beaten	⅓ cup shredded deli roast beef
2 tablespoons water	¾ cup finely shredded low-fat
¼ teaspoon salt	Cheddar cheese
¼ cup diced tomato	

1. In a saucepan over medium-low heat, melt the margarine and add the onion and bell pepper.

2. Stir until the onion and bell pepper are soft but not browned.

3. Add the diced ham and stir until the ham is heated through.

4. Immediately remove from the heat and set the mixture aside.

5. In a mixing bowl, combine the eggs, water, and salt; beat or stir well. Set aside.

6. Heat a 12-inch nonstick skillet over medium-low heat; spray with cooking spray.

7. Pour the egg mixture into the pan and sprinkle with the vegetable and ham mixture, tomato, sausage, bacon, half the roast beef, and ½ cup of the cheese.

8. Cover the pan until the omelet starts to set, 2 to 3 minutes.

9. Immediately remove the lid and fold the omelet from the sides to the middle or in half. Sprinkle with the rest of the roast beef and the remaining ¼ cup cheese.

Serves 2

Calories: 472
Fat: 30.14 grams
Protein: 42.61 grams
Carbohydrates: 7.93 grams
Dietary Fiber: 1.3 grams

The original IHOP version has 1,120 calories per serving. By using diet margarine, turkey meats, and low-fat cheese, you save 648 calories per serving. If you replaced the 4 eggs with 1 cup of egg substitute (such as Egg Beaters), you would save an additional 80 calories per serving.

IHOP
Cream of Wheat Pancakes

3½ cups plain nonfat yogurt
¼ cup honey
One 28-ounce box pancake mix
One 18-ounce box Cream of
   Wheat cereal
2 teaspoons baking powder

5½ cups skim milk
2 cups egg substitute (such as
   Egg Beaters)
8 tablespoons (½ cup) diet
   margarine, melted

1. Mix the yogurt and honey until smooth; cover and set aside in the refrigerator.

2. In a large bowl, combine the pancake mix, Cream of Wheat, and baking powder; set aside.

3. In a separate large bowl, combine the milk, egg substitute, and melted margarine; stir into the dry ingredients and mix until the batter is smooth.

4. For each serving, ladle 3 scant ¼-cup portions of batter onto a medium-hot griddle that has been sprayed with cooking spray. Cook until the pancake tops begin to bubble; flip the pancakes over and cook until golden.

5. Serve each plate with ¼ cup of the yogurt and honey mixture.

Serves 12

NUTRITIONAL INFORMATION (PER SERVING)

Calories: 365
Fat: 10.59 grams
Protein: 19.60 grams
Carbohydrates: 54.58 grams
Dietary Fiber: 6.84 grams

The original IHOP version has 560 calories per serving. By using skim milk, an egg substitute, and diet margarine, you save 195 calories per serving.

IHOP

Pancakes

1¼ cups sifted all-purpose flour	1 egg, beaten
1 teaspoon baking powder	2 tablespoons diet margarine,
1 teaspoon baking soda	melted
Pinch of salt	4 packets Sweet'n Low (or your
1¼ cups skim milk	favorite reduced-calorie sugar
1 tablespoon apple cider vinegar	substitute for cooking)

1. Sift together the flour, baking powder, baking soda, and salt.

2. In a separate bowl, combine the milk with the vinegar and stir. Let sit for about 5 minutes, then whisk in the egg. Add the milk mixture to the flour mixture, stirring just until smooth.

3. Blend in the melted margarine and the sweetener.

4. Cook on a medium-hot griddle sprayed with cooking spray. Use about ¼ cup of batter for each pancake. Ladle the batter onto the griddle in 5-inch-wide circles.

5. Cook until the pancakes are brown on one side and around the edges, then flip and brown the other side.

Serves 4

NUTRITIONAL INFORMATION (PER SERVING)

Calories:	182
Fat:	5.85 grams
Protein:	5.66 grams
Carbohydrates:	27.56 grams
Dietary Fiber:	1.05 grams

The original IHOP version has 320 calories per serving. By making your own buttermilk using skim milk and vinegar and using diet margarine and artificial sweetener, you save 138 calories per serving.

THE IVY
Shepherd's Pie

1 pound lean ground lamb
1 pound extra-lean ground beef
  (95% lean)
Salt and pepper to taste
1 tablespoon diet margarine
½ cup finely chopped onion
2 cloves garlic, crushed
1 teaspoon finely chopped fresh
  thyme

¼ cup all-purpose flour
¼ cup tomato sauce
4 cups beef broth
3 tablespoons Worcestershire
  sauce
¼ cup red wine
4 medium potatoes, boiled, peeled,
  and mashed

1. Mix the ground lamb and ground beef meat together and season with salt and pepper. Place in a large skillet with the margarine and brown, continually breaking up the meat so it will cook uniformly.

2. Remove the meat and sauté the onion, garlic, and thyme until soft.

3. Return the meat to the skillet, sprinkle with the flour, and stir. Add the tomato sauce and cook for a few minutes, stirring constantly.

4. Add the beef broth, Worcestershire sauce, and wine. Bring the mixture to a boil and simmer for 30 to 40 minutes.

5. Drain off most of the liquid and continue to simmer the meat mixture until the remaining liquid has almost evaporated. Remove from the heat and let cool.

6. Preheat the oven to 350°F.

7. Place the meat mixture in a large ovenproof serving dish or in eight individual ovenproof dishes. Top with the mashed potatoes. Bake for 35 to 40 minutes, or until the potatoes are golden brown.

Serves 8

Recipe adapted from
The Ivy: The Restaurant and Its Recipes, *by A.A. Gill*
(London: Hodder & Stoughton, 1999).

Calories: 225
Fat: 16.34 grams
Protein: 24.11 grams
Carbohydrates: 20.79 grams
Dietary Fiber: 2.03 grams

The original version from The Ivy has 452 calories per serving. By using lean meat and browning it in diet margarine and using less wine, you save 227 calories per serving.

JOE'S CRAB SHACK
Crab Cakes

1 egg yolk
⅓ cup fat-free mayonnaise
2½ teaspoons Worcestershire
    sauce
1 teaspoon lemon juice
1 teaspoon dry mustard
1 teaspoon black pepper
¼ teaspoon red pepper flakes
¼ teaspoon Old Bay Seasoning

¼ teaspoon salt
8 slices Sara Lee diet wheat bread,
    toasted
3 tablespoons chopped fresh
    parsley
1 pound lump crabmeat
2 tablespoons diet margarine,
    melted

1. Preheat the oven to 350°F.
2. Beat together the first nine ingredients.
3. Be sure the bread is toasted throughout and dry. Crush into crumbs.
4. Fold the bread crumbs and parsley into the mayonnaise mixture.
5. Break up the crabmeat and then add it to the bread crumb mixture. Form into 4 cakes.
6. Brush each cake on both sides with the melted margarine.
7. Spray a baking sheet with cooking spray. Place the cakes on the baking sheet and bake for 30 to 40 minutes, or until they are light brown.

Serves 4

NUTRITIONAL INFORMATION (PER SERVING)

Calories: 205
Fat: 3.33 grams
Protein: 24.99 grams
Carbohydrates: 14.01 grams
Dietary Fiber: 1.81 grams

The original Joe's Crab Shack version has 410 calories per serving. By using fat-free mayonnaise and diet bread for your crumbs and then baking instead of frying, you cut the calories in half and save 205 calories per serving.

JOE'S CRAB SHACK
Étouffée

1 teaspoon chopped garlic	½ teaspoon cayenne pepper
¾ cup diced onion	½ teaspoon paprika
¼ cup diced celery	¼ teaspoon dry mustard
½ cup diced green bell pepper	½ teaspoon Worcestershire sauce
½ cup chopped mushrooms	8 ounces crawfish meat
3 tablespoons diet margarine	3 tablespoons sliced green onions
1 tablespoon all-purpose flour	1 tablespoon chopped fresh
1½ cups skim milk	parsley
½ teaspoon salt	1½ cups cooked rice

1. Sauté the garlic, onion, celery, bell pepper, and mushrooms in the margarine until soft.

2. Add the flour to the mixture and stir until lightly browned. Stir in the milk and continue stirring until the mixture thickens.

3. Add the salt, cayenne pepper, paprika, dry mustard, Worcestershire sauce, and crawfish meat.

4. Bring to a simmer and continue cooking until the crawfish meat is cooked through.

5. Stir in the green onions and parsley.

6. Scoop ¼ cup of rice into the center of six bowls.

7. Pour the étouffée over the rice.

Serves 6

NUTRITIONAL INFORMATION (PER SERVING)

Calories:	162
Fat:	8.05 grams
Protein:	10.19 grams
Carbohydrates:	21.7 grams
Dietary Fiber:	0.62 gram

The original Joe's Crab Shack version has 330 calories per serving. By using less rice per serving and making your own creamed mixture (versus using canned cream of mushroom and cream of celery soups), you save 168 calories per serving.

JOE'S CRAB SHACK
Harvest Bay Mahimahi

Garlic Butter
6 tablespoons diet margarine
2 cloves garlic, minced

Four 7-ounce mahimahi fillets
Salt and black pepper
½ cup peeled small shrimp
½ cup sliced mushrooms
½ cup skim milk

One 3-ounce package fat-free
  cream cheese, softened
I tablespoon fat-free Parmesan
  cheese
I teaspoon garlic powder
I teaspoon onion powder
I teaspoon white pepper
½ teaspoon minced fresh dill

1. Make the garlic butter ahead of time: Melt the margarine in a small saucepan and add the minced garlic. Simmer over low heat for about 10 minutes. The garlic should be soft and translucent, but do not let the margarine brown. Let cool, and refrigerate in a covered container until ready to use.

2. Preheat the grill to medium heat or preheat the broiler.

3. Season the mahimahi fillets with salt and pepper and cook, turning once, until the fish is cooked through and flakes easily with a fork, 3 to 5 minutes per side. Set aside and keep warm.

4. Melt the garlic butter in a small skillet and sauté the shrimp and mushrooms. (The shrimp will take only a few seconds to cook; the mushrooms should be soft and absorb quite a bit of the melted margarine.)

5. Stir in the milk, cream cheese, Parmesan cheese, garlic powder, onion powder, and white pepper. Heat thoroughly to blend the flavors. Stir in the dill.

6. Place 1 mahimahi fillet on each plate and spoon the shrimp-mushroom sauce over the top. Serve warm.

Serves 4

Calories: 305
Fat: 12.52 grams
Protein: 45.31 grams
Carbohydrates: 3.43 grams
Dietary Fiber: 0.09 gram

The original Joe's Crab Shack version has 570 calories per serving. By using diet margarine and making your own Alfredo sauce, you save 265 calories per serving.

KFC

Original Recipe Fried Chicken (Baked)

I egg, beaten
I cup buttermilk
8 chicken pieces (2 breasts,
2 wings, 2 thighs, 2 drumsticks),
skin removed
6 slices Sara Lee diet wheat bread
¼ teaspoon dried oregano
¼ teaspoon chili powder
¼ teaspoon dried sage

¼ teaspoon dried basil
¼ teaspoon dried marjoram
½ teaspoon pepper
I teaspoon salt
¼ teaspoon paprika
I teaspoon onion salt
I teaspoon garlic powder
I tablespoon Accent

1. Preheat the oven to 350°F.

2. Combine the egg and buttermilk in a large bowl. Soak the skinless chicken pieces in the mixture.

3. Toast the bread until it is dried thoroughly. Crush into bread crumbs. Place the bread crumbs in a separate large bowl and stir in all the herbs and spices.

4. Roll the chicken in the seasoned bread crumbs until completely covered.

5. Place the chicken pieces on a baking sheet that has been sprayed with cooking spray.

6. Bake for 35 to 45 minutes, until cooked through.

Serves 8

NUTRITIONAL INFORMATION (PER SERVING)

	WING	BREAST	DRUMSTICK	THIGH
Calories:	73	187	86	135
Fat:	1.01 grams	3.47 grams	1.80 grams	2.25 grams
Protein:	3.88 grams	16.59 grams	5.20 grams	7.40 grams
Carbohydrates:	6.74 grams	12.75 grams	7.45 grams	10.20 grams
Dietary Fiber:	0.68 gram	1.48 grams	0.82 gram	1.25 grams

The original KFC version has 140 calories for a wing, 320 calories for a breast, 140 calories for a drumstick, and 220 calories for a thigh. By using the diet-bread crumbs and baking instead of frying, you save almost half the calories.

LUBY'S CAFETERIA
Baked Corned Beef Brisket with Sour Cream New Potatoes

4 pounds corned beef brisket
6 packets Sweet'n Low (or your favorite reduced-calorie sugar substitute for cooking)
¼ cup yellow mustard
3 pounds new potatoes, peeled or scrubbed

2 cups fat-free sour cream
6 tablespoons diet margarine, softened
2 teaspoons prepared horseradish
Salt and white pepper

1. Preheat the oven to 225°F.

2. Wrap the corned beef brisket in heavy-duty foil and seal the edges well. Place the brisket in a roasting pan and bake for 3½ hours.

3. Mix the sweetener and mustard together and set aside.

4. Take the brisket out of the oven and increase the temperature to 350°F. Unwrap the brisket and spread the sweetened mustard all over the brisket. Bake, uncovered, for about 15 minutes.

5. While the brisket is baking, cook the potatoes in a pot of boiling water until they are tender, 10 to 15 minutes.

6. Drain the potatoes and mix with the sour cream, margarine, and horseradish, then season with salt and white pepper. Stir gently to coat the potatoes.

7. To serve, thinly slice the brisket against the grain and serve warm with the creamy potatoes.

Serves 10

NUTRITIONAL INFORMATION (PER SERVING)

Calories: 420
Fat: 26.36 grams
Protein: 24.98 grams
Carbohydrates: 21.53 grams
Dietary Fiber: 2.93 grams

The original Luby's Cafeteria version has 890 calories per serving for a larger portion (8 servings), or 595 calories per serving as listed above (10 servings). By using artificial sweetener and fat-free sour cream, and making the portions slightly smaller (from 8 servings to 10 servings), you save 175 calories per serving. (Even with the smaller portions, using the above recipe to serve 10, each person gets about 6½ ounces of meat and about 5 ounces of potatoes.)

LUBY'S CAFETERIA
Fried Catfish (Baked)

¼ cup lemon juice
2 teaspoons Worcestershire sauce
6 slices Sara Lee diet wheat bread, toasted
2 tablespoons paprika
2 tablespoons seasoned salt

Six 7-ounce catfish fillets
Lemon slices and fresh parsley sprigs, for garnish

1. Preheat the oven to 350°F.

2. Whisk together 2 cups of water, the lemon juice, and Worcestershire sauce in a wide, shallow bowl.

3. In another wide, shallow bowl, crumble the toasted bread into crumbs and stir in the paprika and seasoned salt.

4. Dip each fillet in the lemon juice mixture, then in the bread crumb mixture. Place the fillets on a baking sheet that has been sprayed with cooking spray. Sprinkle any remaining bread crumbs on the top of each fillet.

5. Bake for 18 to 20 minutes, until the fish is thoroughly cooked. Remove the fillets by using a spatula to prevent the fish from breaking or tearing.

6. Serve each fillet garnished with lemon and parsley.

Serves 6

NUTRITIONAL INFORMATION (PER SERVING)

Calories:	292
Fat:	12.60 grams
Protein:	35.57 grams
Carbohydrates:	11.38 grams
Dietary Fiber:	5.82 grams

The original Luby's Cafeteria version has 540 calories per serving. By preparing your own bread crumbs and baking instead of frying, you save 248 calories per serving.

LUBY'S CAFETERIA
Smothered Steak with Mushroom Gravy

Steak

⅓ cup all-purpose flour
1 teaspoon salt
½ teaspoon pepper
Six 5-ounce cube steaks
2 tablespoons diet margarine

Gravy

1 tablespoon diet margarine
⅓ cup all-purpose flour
2 cups beef broth
2 tablespoons soy sauce
½ cup skim milk
1 cup thinly sliced mushrooms
Salt and pepper
½ teaspoon minced garlic

1. To prepare the steak, mix the flour with the salt and pepper in a shallow bowl. Lightly coat each steak on both sides.

2. Melt the margarine in a large skillet and fry the steaks, one at a time, turning once, until almost cooked through. Set aside.

3. To make the gravy, in a saucepan, melt the margarine and whisk in the flour. Allow the mixture to begin to simmer slightly. Whisk in the beef broth, soy sauce, and milk and bring to a boil. Reduce the heat and continue to cook, stirring frequently, until the gravy thickens.

4. Add the mushrooms, salt and pepper to taste, and the garlic to the gravy. Continue to simmer on low heat.

5. Preheat the oven to 350°F.

6. Place the steaks in a shallow baking dish that will hold all the steaks in a single layer. (Use two dishes if you don't have one large enough.) Pour half of the gravy over the steaks, and cover the pan with foil. Bake for about 12 minutes.

7. Plate the steaks covering each with some of the gravy. Serve the steaks with the remaining mushroom gravy.

Serves 6

Calories: 342
Fat: 16.93 grams
Protein: 32.56 grams
Carbohydrates: 12.06 grams
Dietary Fiber: 0.48 gram

The original Luby's Cafeteria version has 475 calories per serving. By using less flour and frying in diet margarine instead of oil, you save 133 calories per serving.

MACARONI GRILL
Baked Creamy Seafood

4 tablespoons (¼ cup) diet
margarine
8 ounces bay scallops
3 tablespoons all-purpose flour
1½ cups skim milk
One 3-ounce package fat-free
cream cheese, softened
1½ cups grated low-fat white
Cheddar cheese

2 cups medium shrimp, peeled,
deveined, and cooked
One (6-ounce) can chopped clams,
well drained
2 tablespoons grated low-fat
Parmesan cheese

1. Preheat the oven to 350°F.

2. Over high heat, in a large skillet, melt 1 tablespoon of the margarine;
   add the scallops and stir-fry until just cooked through. Remove from the
   skillet to a bowl and set aside.

3. Using the same skillet, melt the remaining 3 tablespoons margarine over
   medium heat. Whisk in the flour until smooth and bubbly; cook and stir
   for 1 minute.

4. Whisk in the milk and cream cheese. Continue whisking until the
   mixture comes to a boil, then boil, whisking, for 1 minute, or until
   bubbly. Turn off the heat.

5. Whisk in the white Cheddar until melted. Stir in the scallops, shrimp,
   and clams.

6. Transfer the seafood mixture to a 9-inch glass pie plate. Sprinkle with
   the Parmesan cheese and bake for 15 minutes, or until the top is golden
   brown.

Serves 4

Calories: 405
Fat: 12.98 grams
Protein: 54.79 grams
Carbohydrates: 55.90 grams
Dietary Fiber: 0.48 gram

The original Macaroni Grill version has 650 calories per serving. By using diet margarine, skim milk, and low-fat cheeses, you save 245 calories per serving.

MACARONI GRILL
Chicken Scaloppini

Lemon-Butter Sauce
½ cup lemon juice
¼ cup white wine
½ cup skim milk
8 tablespoons (½ cup) diet
margarine
Salt and pepper

Eight 3-ounce boneless, skinless
chicken breasts, pounded thin
Salt and pepper
1 cup all-purpose flour

4 tablespoons (¼ cup) diet
margarine
6 ounces prosciutto, diced
12 ounces mushrooms, sliced
One 12 ounce-jar artichoke hearts,
drained and sliced
1 tablespoon drained capers
1 pound angel hair pasta, cooked
until al dente
Chopped fresh parsley, for garnish

1. To make the sauce, combine the lemon juice and white wine in a small saucepan and reduce by one-third over medium heat. Whisk in the milk and simmer for 3 to 4 minutes. Reduce the heat and add the margarine 1 tablespoon at a time, continuing to whisk as you incorporate it into the mixture. Season with salt and pepper. Remove from the heat and set aside. You can prepare the sauce in advance and refrigerate until ready to use. When you are ready to use, gently reheat over low heat while whisking.

2. Season the chicken breasts with salt and pepper and dredge lightly on both sides with the flour. Melt the margarine in a skillet. Sauté the chicken until cooked through. Remove the chicken once it is done and keep warm.

3. Using the same skillet, add the prosciutto, mushrooms, artichoke hearts, and capers and sauté until the mushrooms are soft. Add half of the lemon-butter sauce to the skillet and gently simmer to coat the vegetables, 1 to 2 minutes.

4. Return the chicken to the pan and turn to coat both sides with the sauce.

5. Plate the cooked pasta and cover each serving with the remaining lemon-butter sauce. Put 1 chicken breast on top of each portion of pasta and pour the pan sauce over the chicken. Garnish with chopped parsley.

Serves 8

NUTRITIONAL INFORMATION (PER SERVING)
Calories: 490
Fat: 14.75 grams
Protein: 29.33 grams
Carbohydrates: 64.45 grams
Dietary Fiber: 22.53 grams

The original Macaroni Grill version has 1,090 calories per serving. By using skim milk, diet margarine, and less flour instead of heavy cream, real butter, and oil for sautéing, you save 600 calories per serving.

MACARONI GRILL
Chocolate Cake with Fudge Sauce

Cake

3½ cups all-purpose flour

1 tablespoon baking soda

1 cup cocoa powder

½ cup sugar

10 packets Sweet'n Low (or your favorite reduced-calorie sugar substitute for cooking)

1 cup egg substitute (such as Egg Beaters)

4 tablespoons (¼ cup) diet margarine, softened

1¾ cups brewed coffee, at room temperature

1½ teaspoons vanilla extract

Fudge Sauce

½ cup skim milk

8 ounces semisweet chocolate chips

Cool Whip Lite topping, for serving

1. Preheat the oven to 350°F. Spray a 13 by 9-inch pan with cooking spray. Lightly coat the pan with a dusting of flour.

2. To make the cake, sift together the flour, baking soda, cocoa powder, sugar, and sweetener into a large bowl.

3. Beat in the egg substitute, margarine, coffee, and vanilla extract, but do not overmix.

4. Pour the batter into the prepared pan.

5. Bake for 25 minutes, or until a toothpick inserted in the center comes out clean. Let the cake cool in the pan for 10 minutes, then remove from the pan and let cool completely on a wire rack.

6. To make the fudge sauce, bring the milk to a simmer in a saucepan over medium heat.

7. Remove from the heat and add the chocolate chips, stirring until they are melted.

8. To serve, place a large square of the cake on each plate. Pour the warm fudge sauce over the cake, and top with a tablespoon of Cool Whip Lite.

Serves 8

NUTRITIONAL INFORMATION (PER SERVING)

Calories: 411
Fat: 14.02 grams
Protein: 11.03 grams
Carbohydrates: 71.07 grams
Dietary Fiber: 6.09 grams

The original Macaroni Grill version has 540 calories per serving, not counting the addition of ice cream and pecans on top. By replacing the sugar with artificial sweetener, the mayonnaise with egg substitute and diet margarine, and the heavy cream with skim milk for the sauce, you save 129 calories per serving.

MACARONI GRILL

Farfalle di Pollo al Sugo Bianco

Cheese Sauce

2 cups skim milk

¼ teaspoon chicken bouillon powder

1 cup shredded low-fat Parmesan cheese

One 3-ounce package fat-free cream cheese, softened

1 tablespoon cornstarch

Pasta

4 tablespoons (¼ cup) diet margarine

½ cup diced red onion

½ cup chopped pancetta

1 tablespoon chopped garlic

¾ cup chopped green onions (green only)

12 ounces grilled chicken, sliced

12 ounces farfalle (bow tie) pasta, cooked until al dente

½ cup skim milk

1 tablespoon chopped fresh parsley, for garnish

1. To make the cheese sauce, heat 1½ cups of the skim milk in a medium saucepan. When it starts to boil slightly, whisk in the chicken bouillon powder and cheeses. Stir the cornstarch into the remaining ½ cup milk and whisk into the cheese sauce. Let the mixture thicken, then remove from the heat and set aside.

2. In a large skillet, melt the margarine and sauté the onion, pancetta, and garlic. Let simmer until the vegetables are just softened. Add the green onions, grilled chicken, and the cooked pasta. Stir in the ½ cup milk and then add the cheese sauce. Stir frequently to blend all the ingredients.

3. Serve the pasta sprinkled with the parsley.

Serves 4

Calories: 635
Fat: 17.50 grams
Protein: 47.98 grams
Carbohydrates: 76.09 grams
Dietary Fiber: 7.10 grams

The original Macaroni Grill version has 1,310 calories per serving. By using skim milk, low-fat cheeses, and diet margarine and slightly decreasing the amount of pasta, you save 675 calories per serving.

MACARONI GRILL
Insalata Florentine

Salad
4 ounces spinach, shredded
4 ounces chilled grilled chicken, sliced
1 ripe plum tomato, diced
2 tablespoons pine nuts, lightly toasted
¼ cup dry-packed sun-dried tomatoes, julienned
2 tablespoons drained capers
¼ cup sliced black olives
¼ cup julienned radicchio
4 ounces cooked orzo pasta, chilled

Dressing
1 tablespoon red wine vinegar
1 tablespoon honey
¼ teaspoon salt
1 teaspoon minced roasted garlic
1 tablespoon olive oil
1 tablespoon lemon juice

Garnish
2 tablespoons grated low-fat Parmesan cheese
Cracked pepper

1. For the salad, toss all the ingredients together in a large bowl.
2. Mix the dressing ingredients together in a small bowl. Pour the dressing over the salad and toss lightly.
3. Garnish the salad with the cheese and cracked pepper.

Serves 4

NUTRITIONAL INFORMATION (PER SERVING)

Calories:	220
Fat:	9.72 grams
Protein:	11.62 grams
Carbohydrates:	18.46 grams
Dietary Fiber:	0.32 gram

The original Macaroni Grill version has 530 calories per serving. By eliminating the oil in the sun-dried tomatoes, using a little less pasta, and using low-fat cheese in the salad, and by using less oil and honey in the dressing, you save 310 calories per serving.

MACARONI GRILL
Pasta Gamberetti e Pinoli

6 tablespoons diet margarine

2 teaspoons minced garlic

½ cup thinly sliced shiitake mushrooms

12 medium shrimp, peeled and deveined

¼ cup dry white wine

¼ cup low-fat sour cream

⅓ cup lemon juice

Salt and white pepper

2 tablespoons plain bread crumbs

5½ cups spinach, washed and dried

4 ounces angel hair pasta, cooked until al dente

1 tablespoon pine nuts, toasted

1. In a large skillet, melt 2 tablespoons of the margarine over medium-high heat. Add the garlic and sauté for about 30 seconds, just enough to make the garlic sizzle. Add the mushrooms and sauté briefly.

2. Add the shrimp and sauté for about 30 seconds, until the shrimp are just half cooked.

3. Add the wine and stir with a wooden spoon to loosen any brown bits on the bottom of the pan. Let cook for 2 minutes, stirring, to finish cooking the shrimp and reduce the liquid. Remove the shrimp mixture in the pan to a warm plate and cover with foil.

4. Add the sour cream to the pan and stir just until warmed. Stir in the lemon juice. Remove the pan from the heat and add the remaining 4 tablespoons margarine, 1 tablespoon at a time, stirring after each addition until melted.

5. Season with salt and white pepper and stir in the bread crumbs. Return the pan to the heat, add the spinach, and cook, stirring, for 1½ minutes, or just until the spinach has wilted.

6. Return the shrimp mixture to the pan and stir to coat and heat through.

7. To serve, divide the angel hair pasta between two warmed serving dishes. Arrange the shrimp on top, spoon the remaining contents of the pan equally over the shrimp, and sprinkle with the toasted pine nuts.

Serves 2

Calories: 525
Fat: 30.39 grams
Protein: 14.43 grams
Carbohydrates: 56.25 grams
Dietary Fiber: 10.2 grams

The original Macaroni Grill version has 960 calories per serving. By using diet margarine, low-fat sour cream, and slightly less pasta per serving, you save 435 calories per serving.

MACARONI GRILL

Polpettone alla Montagona (Italian Meat Loaf)

8 slices Sara Lee diet wheat bread,
toasted
1 cup skim milk
½ cup beef broth
2 pounds extra-lean ground beef
(95% lean)
1 teaspoon salt

½ teaspoon pepper
1 medium onion, diced
1 cup sliced button mushrooms
6 fresh sage leaves, minced
½ cup tomato sauce
½ cup egg substitute (such as
Egg Beaters)

1. Crumble the toasted bread into a medium bowl. Add the milk and beef broth. Allow the bread crumbs to soak up the liquid for about 15 minutes.

2. Using the paddle attachment of a stand mixer, blend the ground beef with the salt, pepper, onion, mushrooms, sage, tomato sauce, and egg substitute on low speed for about 4 minutes. Add the softened bread crumbs and mix for another 4 to 5 minutes.

3. Preheat the oven to 350°F. Spray one large or two smaller loaf pans with cooking spray.

4. Fill the prepared loaf pan with the ground beef mixture. Tap firmly on a solid surface to settle the mixture and release air bubbles. Cover with foil and poke holes for steam to escape.

5. Bake for 1 hour, or until a thermometer inserted into the center of the loaf reaches 165°F. Drain any accumulated liquid. Let the loaf stand for 15 minutes, then carefully invert the pan onto a plate. (The loaf should come out easily and in one piece.) Slice to serve.

Serves 6

Calories: 310
Fat: 8.39 grams
Protein: 43.33 grams
Carbohydrates: 18.62 grams
Dietary Fiber: 7.43 grams

The original Macaroni Grill version has 855 calories per serving. By using skim milk, very lean beef, and tomato sauce instead of ketchup, making your own bread crumbs, and slightly decreasing the portions (which are still over 5 ounces per serving), you save 545 calories per serving.

MACARONI GRILL
Reese's Peanut Butter Cake

Cake

12 tablespoons (¾ cup) diet margarine, softened

¾ cup creamy peanut butter

1 cup packed light brown sugar

8 packets Sweet'n Low (or your favorite reduced-calorie sugar substitute for cooking)

¾ cup egg substitute (such as Egg Beaters)

2 cups all-purpose flour

1 tablespoon baking powder

½ teaspoon salt

1 cup skim milk

1 teaspoon vanilla extract

Peanut Butter Filling

One 8-ounce package fat-free cream cheese, softened

½ cup creamy peanut butter

Chocolate Glaze

½ cup water

4 tablespoons (¼ cup) diet margarine

½ cup cocoa powder

1 cup confectioners' sugar

1 teaspoon vanilla extract

1. Preheat the oven to 350°F. Spray two 9-inch round cake pans with cooking spray. Lightly dust each pan with flour.

2. In a large bowl, cream the margarine and peanut butter until the mixture becomes fluffy. Mix in the brown sugar and sweetener. Add the egg substitute slowly as you mix well.

3. In a small bowl, combine the flour, baking powder, and salt. Add the flour mixture to the peanut butter mixture along with the milk and blend. Add the vanilla extract.

4. Pour the batter into the prepared pans. Bake for about 45 minutes, until a toothpick inserted in the center of each cake comes out clean. After the cake has cooled for 5 minutes, place a covered cake board or cooling rack over the cake and turn the cake over. Gently remove the pan from the cake. Let cool completely before frosting.

5. To make the peanut butter filling, cream the cream cheese and peanut butter until fluffy.

6. Spread half of the filling over the top of each cake. Let chill in the refrigerator.

7. To make the chocolate glaze, combine the water and margarine in a small saucepan. Bring to a boil. Add the cocoa powder, confectioners' sugar, and vanilla extract to the melted margarine. Mix until smooth.

8. Using a metal spatula dipped in water, spread half of the warm chocolate glaze over the peanut butter topping on each cake. The glaze will thicken as it cools.

Makes two 9-inch cakes; serves 12

NUTRITIONAL INFORMATION (PER SERVING)

Calories:	435
Fat:	25.45 grams
Protein:	13.91 grams
Carbohydrates:	68.56 grams
Dietary Fiber:	2.37 grams

The original Macaroni Grill version has 635 calories per serving. By using diet margarine, artificial sweetener instead of some of the sugar, egg substitute, skim milk, and fat-free cream cheese, you retain the full flavor of the peanut butter and chocolate and still save 200 calories per serving.

MACARONI GRILL
Shrimp Portofino

16 medium mushrooms
2 teaspoons chopped garlic
8 tablespoons diet (½ cup)
  margarine, melted
16 large shrimp, peeled and
  deveined
½ teaspoon pepper

3 cloves garlic, minced
¼ cup lemon juice
One 6-ounce jar artichoke hearts,
  drained
2 slices lemon
2 tablespoons chopped fresh
  parsley

1. Sauté the mushrooms and garlic in the melted margarine over medium heat until almost tender, about 5 minutes.

2. Add the shrimp and sauté until the shrimp are cooked, about 3 minutes. Be careful not to overcook the shrimp.

3. Add the pepper, garlic, lemon juice, and artichoke hearts and heat through.

4. Serve over pasta or rice, garnished with the lemon slices and parsley.

Serves 4

NUTRITIONAL INFORMATION (PER SERVING)

Calories:	310
Fat:	14.98 grams
Protein:	9.47 grams
Carbohydrates:	11.69 grams
Dietary Fiber:	7.25 grams

The original Macaroni Grill version has 780 calories per large dinner serving. By using diet margarine, you save 470 calories per large serving.

NOBU
Red Snapper Tempura

½ cup all-purpose flour
2 teaspoons grated lemon zest
1 teaspoon salt
¼ teaspoon black pepper
½ cup lager beer
2 tablespoons diet margarine, melted

1 pound red snapper fillets, cut crosswise into ½-inch-wide strips
Red pepper flakes
4 lemon wedges

1. Preheat the oven to 350°F.
2. Combine the flour, lemon zest, salt, and black pepper in a medium bowl.
3. In a separate medium bowl, whisk the beer and melted margarine together.
4. Dip each fish strip in the beer butter and then in the flour mixture. Lay the fish on a baking sheet that has been sprayed with cooking spray.
5. Bake for 15 to 18 minutes, until brown.
6. Serve with a sprinkle of red pepper flakes and a lemon wedge.

Serves 4

Recipe adapted from StarChefs.com:
The Magazine for Culinary Insiders, Chef Nobu Matsuhisa.

NUTRITIONAL INFORMATION (PER SERVING)

Calories:	228
Fat:	6.91 grams
Protein:	24.84 grams
Carbohydrates:	12.97 grams
Dietary Fiber:	0.43 gram

The original Nobu version has 525 calories per serving. By using a little less batter and baking instead of frying, you save 297 calories per serving.

NOBU

Shrimp, Oyster Mushrooms, and Sugar Snap Peas in Wasabi Butter Sauce

½ cup water
4 teaspoons wasabi powder
2 tablespoons soy sauce
1 ½ teaspoons chicken bouillon powder
1 cup rice wine vinegar
4 tablespoons (¼ cup) diet margarine

4 teaspoons minced garlic
⅔ teaspoon coarsely cracked pepper
4 ounces oyster mushrooms, sliced
16 sugar snap peas, stringed
20 medium shrimp, peeled and deveined
4 cloves garlic, thinly sliced

1. Combine the water, wasabi powder, soy sauce, and bouillon powder. Whisk to blend. Set aside.

2. Bring the rice wine vinegar to a boil in a heavy skillet over medium heat. Allow to reduce to about ¼ cup, about 5 minutes. Add 2 tablespoons of the margarine, the minced garlic, and pepper to the skillet. Add the wasabi mixture to the skillet and boil for about 3 minutes. Set the sauce aside.

3. Melt the remaining 2 tablespoons margarine in a heavy skillet over high heat. Add the mushrooms and peas and sauté for 1 minute. Add the shrimp and sliced garlic and sauté for an additional 2 minutes. Pour the sauce over the shrimp and vegetables and simmer until the shrimp are cooked through and the sauce is slightly thickened, about 1 minute more.

Serves 2

Recipe adapted from StarChefs.com:
The Magazine for Culinary Insiders, Chef Nobu Matsuhisa.

Calories: 325
Fat: 16.10 grams
Protein: 22.17 grams
Carbohydrates: 28.96 grams
Dietary Fiber: 10.15 grams

The original Nobu version has 727 calories per serving. By using diet margarine and fewer oyster mushrooms, you save 402 calories per serving.

O'CHARLEY'S
Potato Soup

8 ounces turkey bacon
2 pounds red potatoes,
scrubbed
4 tablespoons (¼ cup) diet
margarine
½ cup all-purpose flour
3 cups skim milk
2 cups chicken broth

8 ounces light Velveeta
White pepper
Garlic powder
1 teaspoon Tabasco sauce

Garnish
Snipped fresh chives
Chopped fresh parsley

1. Dice the bacon and cook in a skillet until all the fat is rendered. Drain the bacon and set aside until ready to use.

2. Cut the potatoes into ½-inch dice and place in a pot with water to cover. Boil for 10 minutes, drain, and set aside.

3. Melt the margarine in a heavy pot and add the flour, whisking constantly until the paste is smooth. Gradually add the milk and chicken broth, whisking constantly. When the sauce begins to thicken, add the Velveeta, whisking frequently.

4. When the Velveeta is melted completely and the sauce is smooth, add the potatoes. Season to taste with white pepper and garlic powder. Add the Tabasco. Lower the heat and simmer, covered, for 30 minutes, stirring occasionally.

5. Ladle the soup into bowls and garnish with the bacon bits, chives, and parsley.

Serves 8

Calories: 307
Fat: 9.84 grams
Protein: 15.26 grams
Carbohydrates: 41.21 grams
Dietary Fiber: 4.30 grams

The original O'Charley's version has 380 calories per serving. By using turkey bacon, diet margarine, skim milk, and light Velveeta, you save 73 calories per serving.

THE OLD SPAGHETTI FACTORY
Spaghetti with Browned Butter and Cheese

8 tablespoons (1 stick) butter
8 tablespoons (½ cup) diet margarine
12 ounces whole wheat spaghetti, cooked until al dente

½ cup low-fat ricotta cheese
½ cup shredded low-fat mozzarella cheese
Salt and pepper

1. Melt the butter and margarine together in a small saucepan over medium heat. Bring the mixture to an easy boil. The solids will sink to the bottom of the saucepan and begin to brown. The boiling process evaporates the water, so you are left with the toasted solids and the butter and vegetable fats. This process will take 5 to 10 minutes. Remove from the heat and set aside.

2. Toss the hot spaghetti with the browned butter and the cheeses. Season with salt and pepper.

Serves 4

NUTRITIONAL INFORMATION (PER SERVING)
Calories: 680
Fat: 43.08 grams
Protein: 19.76 grams
Carbohydrates: 65.92 grams
Dietary Fiber: 2.73 grams

The original Old Spaghetti Factory version has 1,040 calories per serving. By using diet margarine in place of some of the butter, using whole wheat spaghetti, and replacing the goat cheese with low-fat cheeses, you save 360 calories per serving.

OLIVE GARDEN
Cheese Ravioli with Vegetables

2 tablespoons diet margarine
1 clove garlic, chopped
One 7-ounce jar roasted red peppers, drained and sliced into strips
½ cup julienned dry-packed sun-dried tomatoes
½ cup sliced pitted black olives
1 medium zucchini, diced
1 cup chicken broth
Salt and pepper
1 pound cheese ravioli, cooked according to the package directions
Chopped fresh parsley, for garnish

1. In a large saucepan, melt the margarine and sauté the garlic with the roasted red peppers, sun-dried tomatoes, olives, and zucchini. When the zucchini is crisp-tender, add the chicken broth and season with salt and pepper. Simmer for 2 minutes.

2. Add the cooked ravioli to the sauce and simmer for a few minutes to heat through, tossing the ravioli gently to coat them with the sauce.

3. Transfer to a serving platter and garnish with the parsley.

Serves 4

NUTRITIONAL INFORMATION (PER SERVING)

Calories: 446
Fat: 14.40 grams
Protein: 14.13 grams
Carbohydrates: 39.63 grams
Dietary Fiber: 3.65 grams

The original Olive Garden version has 660 calories per serving. By using diet margarine and sun-dried tomatoes with no oil and eliminating the cheese on top of the dish, you save 214 calories per serving.

OLIVE GARDEN
Chicken Crostina

Crust

6 slices Sara Lee diet wheat bread

¼ cup grated low-fat Parmesan cheese

4 tablespoons (¼ cup) diet margarine, melted

½ teaspoon garlic powder

¼ cup chopped fresh parsley

1 small potato, peeled and grated

Salt and pepper

1½ cups all-purpose flour

1 tablespoon salt

1 tablespoon pepper

1 tablespoon Italian seasoning

6 boneless, skinless chicken breasts

12 ounces whole wheat linguine

1 tablespoon diet margarine

1 tablespoon roasted garlic, minced

1 tablespoon all-purpose flour

1 cup white wine

1½ cups skim milk

1 cup grated low-fat Parmesan cheese

1 cup diced ripe Roma tomatoes

2 tablespoons chopped fresh parsley, for garnish

1. Preheat the oven to 350°F.

2. Make the crust: Toast the bread until dry throughout and crumble into crumbs. Mix the bread crumbs with the Parmesan cheese, melted margarine, garlic powder, parsley, potato, and salt and pepper to taste. Set aside.

3. Mix the flour, salt, pepper, and Italian seasoning in a shallow dish. Dredge the chicken with the mixture, shaking off any excess.

4. Place the chicken on a baking sheet that has been sprayed with cooking spray. Bake at 375°F for 30 minutes, or until the internal temperature of the chicken reaches 165°F.

5. Remove the chicken from the oven and top with the potato crust mixture. Turn the oven setting to broil and place the chicken back in the oven. Broil until the crust is golden brown, 1 to 2 minutes.

6. Cook the linguine according to the package directions. Drain and set aside.

7. Melt the margarine in a saucepan. Add the roasted garlic and cook for 1 minute. Stir in the 1 tablespoon flour. Add the wine and bring to a

boil. Add the milk, Parmesan cheese, and tomatoes. The sauce is done when it is bubbling throughout and begins to thicken.

8. Coat the pasta with some of the sauce, then serve topped with the chicken and the remaining sauce. Garnish with the parsley.

Serves 6

NUTRITIONAL INFORMATION (PER SERVING)

Calories:	675
Fat:	13.73 grams
Protein:	44.97 grams
Carbohydrates:	79.88 grams
Dietary Fiber:	9.08 grams

The original Olive Garden version has 1,040 calories per serving. By using low-fat cheese, diet margarine, and skim milk, and only 2 ounces of linguine per serving, you save 365 calories per serving.

OLIVE GARDEN
Chicken Marsala

¼ cup Wondra or cake flour
½ teaspoon salt
½ teaspoon pepper
½ teaspoon dried oregano
4 boneless, skinless chicken
  breasts

4 tablespoons (¼ cup) diet
  margarine, melted
1 cup sliced mushrooms
½ cup Marsala wine

1. Preheat the oven to 350°F.

2. In a shallow dish, combine the flour, salt, pepper, and oregano. Stir to blend.

3. Coat the chicken breasts with the melted margarine. Dredge each piece with the seasoned flour. Save the leftover melted margarine and seasoned flour.

4. Place the chicken on a baking sheet that has been sprayed with cooking spray.

5. Bake for 25 to 30 minutes, until no longer pink.

6. Pour the reserved margarine into a large skillet. Mix 1 tablespoon of the reserved seasoned flour into the margarine. Stir until lightly browned.

7. Add the mushrooms to the skillet. When the mushrooms are heated thoroughly, add the wine and stir.

8. Place the cooked breasts in the skillet with the mushroom sauce. Cover and simmer for about 10 minutes, until the chicken is cooked through.

9. Serve the chicken with the mushroom sauce spooned over the top.

Serves 4

Calories: 275
Fat: 10.34 grams
Protein: 28.23 grams
Carbohydrates: 9.67 grams
Dietary Fiber: 0.39 gram

The original Olive Garden version is served on a bed of linguine and has 770 calories per serving. By baking the chicken instead of frying it, you get only 275 calories per serving rather than 559. If you add a 2-ounce serving of linguine, the total calories are 486 and you still save 284 calories per serving.

OLIVE GARDEN
Chicken Scampi

10 cloves garlic, peeled
1 tablespoon diet margarine

White Sauce
1 tablespoon diet margarine
2 tablespoons all-purpose flour
¾ cup hot skim milk

Scampi Sauce Base
3 tablespoons diet margarine
2 tablespoons crushed garlic
2 tablespoons Italian seasoning

Black pepper
¾ teaspoon red pepper flakes
¼ cup white wine
1½ cups chicken broth

2 boneless, skinless chicken
  breasts, sliced
1 red bell pepper, julienned
1 red onion, thinly sliced
8 ounces angel hair pasta, cooked
  until al dente

1. Preheat the oven to 400°F.

2. In a small ovenproof saucepan, sauté the garlic cloves in the margarine. Put the pan in the oven for 20 to 30 minutes, until the cloves feel soft when pressed, or cover and slowly roast on the stove top over low heat. Be sure the garlic does not burn, as burning will make it taste bitter. Remove the garlic and save the margarine.

3. Make the white sauce: In a small saucepan, melt the margarine and whisk in the flour, stirring constantly until the paste is smooth. Gradually add the hot milk, whisking constantly. Simmer until the sauce has thickened. Set aside.

4. Make the scampi sauce base: In another saucepan, melt the margarine and add the crushed garlic, the Italian seasoning, black pepper, and the red pepper flakes. Cook for about 2 minutes over low heat, then add the wine and chicken broth. Simmer for about 30 minutes.

5. Add ¼ cup of the white sauce to the scampi sauce base and whisk to combine all the ingredients. Simmer until the liquid has thickened.

6. Heat the reserved melted margarine in a large saucepan and sauté the chicken until it is almost cooked through. Add the bell pepper and onion and continue to sauté. When the chicken is cooked through and no longer pink in the middle, add the scampi sauce. Simmer until

everything is warmed and then add the roasted garlic cloves. Plate the pasta in serving bowls or plates and pour the chicken, vegetables, and sauce over the top.

Serves 2

NUTRITIONAL INFORMATION (PER SERVING)

Calories:	820
Fat:	22.98 grams
Protein:	47.18 grams
Carbohydrates:	105.50 grams
Dietary Fiber:	6.70 grams

The original Olive Garden version has 1,070 calories per serving. By using diet margarine, skim milk, and less white wine, you save 250 calories per serving. If you divided this recipe into 4 servings (which would still be 2 ounces of pasta per serving), you would cut the calorie count down to 410 per serving.

OLIVE GARDEN

Italian Sausage–Stuffed Portobello Mushrooms with Herb and Parmesan Cheese Sauce

Cream Sauce
1½ cups skim milk
One 3-ounce package fat-free cream cheese, softened
¼ cup grated low-fat Parmesan cheese
2 tablespoons chopped fresh basil
Salt and pepper

Stuffing
½ cup egg substitute (such as Egg Beaters)
¼ cup skim milk
1 teaspoon chopped fresh parsley
1 teaspoon chopped fresh basil
1 teaspoon chopped fresh marjoram
1 clove garlic, chopped
4 slices Sara Lee diet wheat bread, toasted
¼ cup grated low-fat Parmesan cheese
8 ounces bulk turkey sausage
4 large portobello mushrooms
Chopped fresh parsley, for garnish

1. To make the cream sauce, bring the milk to a gentle boil and whisk in the cream cheese. Allow the mixture to simmer for about 5 minutes. Add the Parmesan cheese, basil, and salt and pepper. Set aside.

2. Prepare the stuffing by whisking the egg substitute with the milk in a large bowl. Add the parsley, basil, marjoram, and garlic. Cut the toasted bread into small croutons and stir into the egg mixture, along with the Parmesan cheese. Set aside.

3. Sauté the sausage in a skillet, breaking it up as it cooks. When it is thoroughly browned, remove it with a slotted spoon and add it to the stuffing mixture, stirring well to combine.

4. Preheat the oven to 350°F.

5. Remove the stems and the spongy undersides of the mushrooms so that the caps resemble hollowed-out bowls. Place the caps, open side down, on a baking sheet and bake for about 8 minutes, until they are a little soft.

6. Stuff the mushroom caps with the sausage mixture and put them back in the oven to bake for 15 to 20 minutes, until they are golden brown on top and cooked through. To serve, spoon the cream sauce over each mushroom and garnish with the chopped parsley.

Serves 4

Note: Parsley flakes and dried basil and marjoram may be used in the stuffing if you decrease the amount to ½ teaspoon each.

NUTRITIONAL INFORMATION (PER SERVING)

Calories:	220
Fat:	8.28 grams
Protein:	41.14 grams
Carbohydrates:	20.32 grams
Dietary Fiber:	6.10 grams

The original Olive Garden version has 280 calories per serving. By using skim milk and low-fat cheeses and making your own croutons, you save 60 calories per serving.

OLIVE GARDEN
Pasta Frittata

4 ounces turkey bacon, diced

Frittata Batter

1 ½ cups egg substitute (such as Egg Beaters)

2 cups skim milk

5 teaspoons cornstarch

Salt and white pepper

Pinch of nutmeg (optional)

8 ounces spaghetti, broken into 2-inch pieces, cooked until al dente

¼ cup sliced green onions

¼ cup grated low-fat Parmesan cheese

1. Sauté the bacon until it is cooked through. Drain on paper towels and set aside.

2. Preheat the oven to 350°F. Spray a 1½-quart baking dish with cooking spray and set aside.

3. To make the frittata batter, beat together the egg substitute, milk, cornstarch, salt and white pepper, and nutmeg, if desired.

4. Combine the cooked spaghetti with the green onions, bacon, and ¼ teaspoon white pepper. Mix well and transfer to the prepared baking dish. Pour the frittata batter over the spaghetti and bake for 25 minutes, or until the center is firm.

5. Sprinkle with the cheese, return to the oven, and bake just until the cheese is golden brown. Turn off the heat and open the oven door to let the frittata dry out a little. (This will make it firm enough to slice.)

6. Slice and serve.

Serves 2

NUTRITIONAL INFORMATION (PER SERVING)

Calories: 735

Fat: 13.18 grams

Protein: 47.33 grams

Carbohydrates: 128.76 grams

Dietary Fiber: 10.05 grams

The original Olive Garden version has 1,625 calories per serving. By using turkey bacon, egg substitute, skim milk, and low-fat cheese and slightly decreasing the amount of pasta, you save 890 calories per serving. (Using skim milk instead of half-and-half saves you almost 300 calories per serving!)

OLIVE GARDEN
Risotto Milanese

4 tablespoons (¼ cup) diet
   margarine
½ cup finely chopped onion
½ teaspoon ground turmeric
½ cup sliced mushrooms
5 cups chicken broth

1½ cups long-grain white rice
¼ cup white wine
½ cup grated low-fat Parmesan
   cheese
Salt and pepper
Chopped fresh parsley, for garnish

1. Melt 2 tablespoons of the margarine in a stockpot over medium heat and sauté the onion and turmeric until the onion is soft. Add the mushrooms and sauté until they absorb some of the liquid.

2. Heat the broth in a saucepan and keep warm.

3. Add the rice to the sautéed vegetables and stir until all the grains are coated with the margarine mixture. Add the white wine and let it evaporate, stirring frequently.

4. Add the warm broth, ½ cup at a time, allowing it to be absorbed after each addition, stirring constantly. Repeat this procedure until all the broth is absorbed and the rice is al dente.

5. Remove the pan from the heat and add the cheese and the remaining 2 tablespoons margarine. Mix gently as you add these ingredients. Season with salt and pepper. Transfer to a serving dish and garnish with parsley.

Serves 4

NUTRITIONAL INFORMATION (PER SERVING)

Calories: 330
Fat: 10.53 grams
Protein: 10.89 grams
Carbohydrates: 59.88 grams
Dietary Fiber: 2.20 grams

The original Olive Garden version has 525 calories per serving. By using diet margarine and low-fat cheese, you save 195 calories per serving.

OLIVE GARDEN
Shrimp Cristoforo

16 tablespoons (1 cup) diet
margarine, softened
1 teaspoon minced garlic
Salt and pepper
½ cup grated low-fat Monterey
Jack cheese

¼ cup finely chopped fresh basil
1 pound medium shrimp, peeled
and deveined
1 pound linguine, cooked until al
dente

1. Use a hand mixer to beat the margarine, garlic, and salt and pepper until smooth and creamy. Add the cheese and basil.

2. Transfer the flavored margarine to a skillet and add the shrimp. Sauté for a minute or two, until the shrimp are pink and cooked through.

3. Put the warm pasta in a large bowl and pour the sauce over the top.

Serves 4

NUTRITIONAL INFORMATION (PER SERVING)
Calories: 750
Fat: 33.90 grams
Protein: 34.18 grams
Carbohydrates: 86.25 grams
Dietary Fiber: 3.65 grams

The original Olive Garden version has 1,150 calories per serving. By using diet margarine and low-fat cheese, you save 400 calories per serving. (If you made the portions smaller and served 6 from this recipe, you would save over 600 calories per serving and still have over 2½ ounces of pasta and 2½ ounces of shrimp per serving.)

OLIVE GARDEN
Tuscan Garlic Chicken

1 tablespoon salt	1 red bell pepper, julienned
2 teaspoons pepper	1 tablespoon all-purpose flour
1 teaspoon dried marjoram	$\frac{1}{2}$ cup dry white wine
1 teaspoon chopped fresh basil	8 ounces spinach, stemmed
1 teaspoon dried oregano	1 $\frac{1}{2}$ cups skim milk
6 boneless, skinless chicken	1 cup grated low-fat Parmesan
breasts	cheese
1 tablespoon diet margarine	1 pound fettuccine, cooked until al
1 tablespoon chopped garlic	dente

1. Preheat the oven to 350°F.

2. Combine the salt, pepper, marjoram, basil, and oregano in a small bowl. Sprinkle the mixture on both sides of each chicken breast. Place the chicken on a baking sheet coated with cooking spray. Place in the oven and cook for about 25 minutes, until cooked through.

3. Melt the margarine in a saucepan and sauté the garlic and bell pepper. When the garlic is soft, start whisking in the flour, stirring constantly until the flour is smooth and slightly browned.

4. Add the wine to the saucepan and bring to a low boil. Add the spinach and milk and stir until the spinach is just wilted. Stir in the Parmesan cheese.

5. Toss the pasta with half of the cheese sauce and transfer to a warmed serving bowl. Put some pasta on each plate and top with a chicken breast, then pour some of the remaining sauce over the top.

Serves 6

Calories: 520
Fat: 7.86 grams
Protein: 41.35 grams
Carbohydrates: 63.14 grams
Dietary Fiber: 3.72 grams

The original Olive Garden version has 860 calories per serving. By using diet margarine, skim milk, and low-fat cheese, and baking the chicken instead of frying it, you save 340 calories per serving.

OUTBACK STEAKHOUSE
Aussie Cheese Fries

Dipping Sauce
½ cup fat-free sour cream
1 tablespoon horseradish
Pinch of cayenne pepper
Pinch of salt
Pinch of black pepper

One 1-pound bag frozen French fries

4 tablespoons (¼ cup) diet margarine
Salt
1 cup shredded low-fat Colby-Jack cheese
6 slices turkey bacon, cooked and crumbled

1. Make the dipping sauce: Combine all the sauce ingredients and blend well. Cover and refrigerate until ready to serve.
2. Preheat the oven to 350°F.
3. Place the fries on a baking sheet that has been sprayed with cooking spray. Melt the margarine and sprinkle over the fries. Be sure all the fries have some of the margarine.
4. Bake the fries for 20 to 25 minutes, until brown and crispy.
5. Salt the fries to taste and sprinkle with the cheese and bacon.
6. Place the fries back in the oven and leave just until the cheese begins to melt.
7. Serve with the dipping sauce.

Serves 6

Calories: 210
Fat: 11.39 grams
Protein: 8.68 grams
Carbohydrates: 20.07 grams
Dietary Fiber: 1.42 grams

The original Outback Steakhouse version has 353 calories per serving. By using diet margarine, low-fat cheese, and turkey bacon, and baking the potatoes instead of frying them, you save 143 calories per serving.

OUTBACK STEAKHOUSE
Mac a Roo 'n' Cheese

3 tablespoons diet margarine
2 tablespoons all-purpose flour
1½ cups skim milk
¼ teaspoon salt
⅛ teaspoon paprika
½ cup grated low-fat Parmesan
  cheese

One 3-ounce package fat-free
  cream cheese
12 ounces medium rigatoni,
  cooked until al dente

1. Melt the margarine in a medium saucepan and whisk in the flour, stirring to thicken. When the mixture is smooth, whisk in the milk, salt, and paprika, then incorporate the cheeses until the sauce is smooth and thick.

2. Add the cooked pasta to the sauce and serve warm.

Serves 3

NUTRITIONAL INFORMATION (PER SERVING)

Calories:	580
Fat:	12.44 grams
Protein:	25.04 grams
Carbohydrates:	94.65 grams
Dietary Fiber:	3.77 grams

The original Outback Steakhouse version has 680 calories per serving. By using diet margarine, skim milk, and low-fat cheeses, you save 100 calories per serving. If you made the servings slightly smaller (3 ounces of pasta each instead of 4 ounces), there would be 435 calories per serving and you would save 245 calories per serving.

PANDA EXPRESS
Garlic Chicken Breasts with String Beans

2 tablespoons soy sauce
2 teaspoons rice wine vinegar
1 teaspoon Asian sesame oil
2 teaspoons cornstarch
1 packet Sweet'n Low (or your favorite reduced-calorie sugar substitute for cooking)
1 pound boneless, skinless chicken breasts, cut into ¼-inch strips
2 tablespoons diet margarine

1 large onion, peeled and cut into ½-inch wedges
2 tablespoons minced garlic
1 teaspoon black bean sauce
12 ounces green beans, cut into 3-inch pieces
1 cup coarsely diced red bell pepper
¼ cup water

1. Combine the soy sauce, vinegar, sesame oil, cornstarch, and sweetener. Whisk to blend. Add the chicken strips and toss to coat well. Refrigerate, covered, for about 20 minutes.

2. Melt the margarine in a wok or large skillet and stir-fry the chicken for about 3 minutes, until the chicken begins to brown and is cooked through. Remove the chicken from the wok and keep warm.

3. Add the onion, garlic, and black bean sauce to the wok. Stir in the green beans and bell pepper. Add the water, cover, and cook for 3 minutes, or until the vegetables are crisp-tender. Return the chicken to the wok and stir-fry quickly to combine the flavors.

Serves 6

NUTRITIONAL INFORMATION (PER SERVING)

Calories:	140
Fat:	4.53 grams
Protein:	17.55 grams
Carbohydrates:	8.82 grams
Dietary Fiber:	2.52 grams

The original Panda Express version has 190 calories per serving. By using artificial sweetener and diet margarine, you save 50 calories per serving.

PANDA EXPRESS
Spicy Chicken

½ cup diced chayote squash or zucchini

2 tablespoons diet margarine

12 ounces boneless, skinless chicken breasts, diced

Salt and black pepper

⅓ cup diced onion

¼ cup diced red bell pepper

8 pieces whole dried chile pepper

½ teaspoon minced fresh ginger

½ teaspoon minced garlic

1½ teaspoons red pepper flakes

½ teaspoon Shao hsing wine (rice wine)

1 teaspoon soy sauce

2 tablespoons chicken broth

1 packet Sweet'n Low (or your favorite reduced-calorie sugar substitute for cooking)

1 tablespoon cornstarch

1 tablespoon roasted peanuts

1. Blanch the squash for 1 minute in a steamer or boiling water. Drain and set aside.

2. Melt the margarine in a wok or large skillet and add the diced chicken; season with salt and black pepper. Stir-fry until the chicken is cooked through, then add the onion and bell pepper and cook until the vegetables are crisp-tender. Remove the vegetables with the chicken and set aside.

3. Leave any juices and margarine in the wok and add the chile pepper, ginger, and garlic and cook until slightly soft. Add the red pepper flakes, wine, soy sauce, chicken broth, and sweetener. Bring to a boil and whisk in the cornstarch.

4. Add the cooked chicken mixture and the blanched squash and toss with the other ingredients to combine. Toss in the peanuts and serve warm.

Serves 2

Calories: 270
Fat: 13.81 grams
Protein: 41.65 grams
Carbohydrates: 6.21 grams
Dietary Fiber: 0.85 gram

The original Panda Express version has 300 calories per serving. By using diet margarine and artificial sweetener, you save 30 calories per serving.

PANERA BREAD
Apple-Sausage Patties with Sage

2 tablespoons finely chopped onion
1 Granny Smith apple, peeled and finely diced
1 teaspoon olive oil
3 cloves garlic, minced
½ teaspoon ground ginger
1 teaspoon minced fresh thyme, or ½ teaspoon dried
1 tablespoon minced fresh sage, or 1 teaspoon dried
¼ teaspoon salt
¼ teaspoon pepper
1 pound coarsely ground lean turkey
1 egg white, beaten
6 slices Sara Lee diet wheat bread
Dijon mustard, for serving

1. Sauté the onion and apple in the olive oil until just softened. Add the garlic, ginger, herbs, salt, and pepper. Set aside to cool before using.

2. Once cooled, combine the apple mixture with the ground turkey and the egg white. Blend the mixture well, making sure the egg white is evenly distributed. Shape into 12 patties.

3. Heat a nonstick skillet and sauté the patties until they are cooked through, turning once, 2 to 3 minutes on each side.

4. Lightly toast the bread. Cut each slice into 4 pieces, making 24 pieces. Place one patty between 2 pieces of toasted bread. Serve the Dijon mustard on the side.

Serves 12

Calories: 95
Fat: 8.16 grams
Protein: 9.88 grams
Carbohydrates: 7.02 grams
Dietary Fiber: 2.89 grams

The original Panera Bread version has 275 calories per serving. By using ground turkey instead of pork and using diet bread instead of sourdough bread, you save 180 calories per serving.

PANERA BREAD
Broccoli-Cheese Soup

½ medium onion, chopped
3 tablespoons diet margarine, melted
¼ cup all-purpose flour
2 cups skim milk
2 cups chicken broth
8 ounces broccoli, coarsely chopped
1 cup shredded carrots
Salt and pepper
1 cup grated low-fat sharp Cheddar cheese
One 3-ounce package fat-free cream cheese, softened
¼ teaspoon ground nutmeg

1. Sauté the onion in 1 tablespoon of the melted margarine. Set aside.

2. Using a wire whisk, combine the remaining 2 tablespoons melted margarine and the flour in a large pot over medium heat. Cook, stirring frequently, for about 4 minutes.

3. Slowly add the milk and continue stirring. Add the chicken broth, whisking all the time. Simmer for 20 minutes.

4. Add the broccoli, carrots, and sautéed onion. Cook over low heat until the vegetables are tender, about 20 minutes.

5. Add salt and pepper to taste.

6. By now the soup should be thickened. Pour in batches into a blender and puree.

7. Return the puree to the pot and place over low heat. Add the grated cheese and the cream cheese and stir until well blended. Stir in the nutmeg.

Serves 4

Calories: 232
Fat: 11.17 grams
Protein: 18.41 grams
Carbohydrates: 24.89 grams
Dietary Fiber: 3.63 grams

The original Panera Bread version has 290 calories per serving. By using diet margarine, skim milk, low-fat Cheddar, and fat-free cream cheese, you save 58 calories per serving.

PANERA BREAD
Chicken Breasts
with Herbed Crust

8 boneless, skinless chicken breasts
½ cup lemon juice
8 slices Sara Lee diet wheat bread, toasted
⅓ cup chopped fresh basil
¼ cup chopped fresh parsley

2 tablespoons chopped fresh rosemary
1½ teaspoons salt
½ teaspoon pepper
3 tablespoons diet margarine, melted
Lemon wedges, for garnish

1. Using the flat side of a meat mallet, pound each chicken breast between 2 sheets of plastic wrap to a thickness of about ½ inch. Place the breasts in a shallow bowl. Pour the lemon juice over the chicken and refrigerate, covered, for 1 hour.

2. Crumble the toasted bread into bread crumbs and combine with the basil, parsley, rosemary, salt, and pepper; set aside.

3. Preheat the oven to 450°F. Line a baking sheet with foil and spray with cooking spray.

4. Take the breasts out of the lemon juice and pat dry. Brush each breast with the melted margarine, then coat both sides with the seasoned bread crumbs. Lay the breasts on the prepared baking sheet and bake for about 20 minutes, until the crust is golden and the chicken is cooked through.

5. Serve with lemon wedges.

Serves 8

NUTRITIONAL INFORMATION (PER SERVING)

Calories: 210
Fat: 6.18 grams
Protein: 30.05 grams
Carbohydrates: 10 grams
Dietary Fiber: 5 grams

The original Panera Bread version has 325 calories per serving. By using diet bread to make your own bread crumbs and using diet margarine, you save 115 calories per serving.

P.F. CHANG'S CHINA BISTRO
Chicken-Lettuce Wraps

8 dried shiitake mushrooms
4 teaspoons hoisin sauce
2 teaspoons soy sauce
3 teaspoons dry sherry
2 teaspoons oyster sauce
4 teaspoons water
5 tablespoons diet margarine, melted
1 packet Sweet'n Low (or your favorite reduced-calorie sugar substitute for cooking)
3 teaspoons cornstarch
Salt and pepper

1 pound boneless, skinless chicken breasts, cut into thin strips
1 teaspoon minced peeled fresh ginger
2 cloves garlic, minced
2 small dried chiles
2 green onions, minced
1 cup minced bamboo shoots
1 cup minced water chestnuts
1 cup cooked cellophane noodles
1 head iceberg lettuce, separated into leaves, for wrapping

1. Cover the mushrooms with boiling water; let stand for 30 minutes and then drain. Remove and discard the woody stems. Mince the mushrooms and set aside.

2. Mix together the hoisin sauce, 1 teaspoon of the soy sauce, 1 teaspoon of the sherry, the oyster sauce, 2 teaspoons of the water, 1 tablespoon of the margarine, the sweetener, and 2 teaspoons of the cornstarch. Set the sauce aside.

3. In a medium bowl, combine the remaining 1 teaspoon cornstarch, 2 teaspoons sherry, 2 teaspoons water, 1 teaspoon soy sauce, salt and pepper to taste, and the chicken. Stir to coat the chicken thoroughly and let marinate for 15 minutes.

4. Place 3 tablespoons of the margarine in a wok or large skillet over medium-high heat. Add the chicken and stir-fry for 3 to 4 minutes. Remove from the pan and set aside.

5. Add the remaining 1 tablespoon margarine to the pan. Add the ginger, garlic, chiles, and green onions. Stir-fry for about 1 minute.

6. Add the minced mushrooms, bamboo shoots, and water chestnuts; stir-fry for an additional 2 minutes. Return the chicken to the pan.

7. Add the sauce to the pan and cook until thickened and hot.

8. Break the cooked cellophane noodles into small pieces and place on the bottom of a serving dish. Pour the chicken mixture on top of the noodles. Serve with lettuce leaves for wrapping.

Makes about 12 wraps

NUTRITIONAL INFORMATION (PER WRAP)

Calories:	140
Fat:	3.94 grams
Protein:	5.16 grams
Carbohydrates:	17.24 grams
Dietary Fiber:	1.52 grams

The original P.F. Chang's China Bistro version has 160 calories per wrap. By using diet margarine and artificial sweetener, you save 20 calories per wrap.

P.F. CHANG'S CHINA BISTRO

Chicken with Black Bean Sauce

½ cup water

2 teaspoons rice wine or dry sherry

2 teaspoons mushroom soy sauce

2 teaspoons oyster sauce

2 packets Sweet'n Low (or your favorite reduced-calorie sugar substitute for cooking)

2 tablespoons cornstarch

4 boneless, skinless chicken breasts

¼ cup egg substitute (such as Egg Beaters)

4 tablespoons (¼ cup) diet margarine, melted

1 teaspoon minced fresh ginger

2 teaspoons fermented black beans

1 tablespoon minced green onion

½ teaspoon minced garlic

1½ cups chicken broth

Pinch of white pepper

1. Mix together the water, rice wine, soy sauce, oyster sauce, 1 packet of the sweetener, and 1 tablespoon of the cornstarch. Stir well until the cornstarch is incorporated.

2. Cut the chicken breasts into strips.

3. Combine the egg substitute, 2 tablespoons of the margarine, and the remaining 1 tablespoon cornstarch in a medium bowl. Add the chicken strips in batches and coat on all sides with the egg mixture.

4. Heat a wok or large skillet. Add the remaining 2 tablespoons margarine, then the chicken, and cook until the chicken is opaque all over.

5. Remove the chicken. Add the ginger, black beans, and green onion to the pan and stir-fry. Add the chicken strips and garlic. Then add the sauce you prepared in step 1 and the chicken broth. Add the remaining 1 packet sweetener and the white pepper. Stir-fry briefly after each addition to keep things mixed well.

6. Cook just until the sauce is thickened and all of the ingredients are combined well.

Serves 4

Calories: 205
Fat: 6.6 grams
Protein: 27.52 grams
Carbohydrates: 4.54 grams
Dietary Fiber: 1.01 grams

The original P.F. Chang's China Bistro version has 300 calories per serving. By using artificial sweetener and diet margarine, you save 95 calories per serving.

P.F. CHANG'S CHINA BISTRO
Ginger Chicken with Broccoli

Chicken
½ cup egg substitute (such as Egg Beaters)
¼ teaspoon white pepper
¼ teaspoon salt
1 pound boneless, skinless chicken breasts, sliced

Stir-Fry Sauce
½ cup soy sauce
2 tablespoons rice wine vinegar
6 packets Sweet'n Low (or your favorite reduced-calorie sugar substitute for cooking)
½ cup chicken broth

3 cups chicken broth
8 ounces broccoli florets
2 tablespoons diet margarine
2 tablespoons minced peeled fresh ginger
2 tablespoons minced green onion
1 teaspoon minced garlic
¼ cup cornstarch
½ cup water
1 teaspoon Asian sesame oil

1. Marinate the chicken ahead of time: Combine the egg substitute, white pepper, and salt. Add the chicken pieces and marinate, covered, in the refrigerator for at least 3 hours. Drain well when ready to use. Discard the marinade.

2. Make the stir-fry sauce: Combine the soy sauce, vinegar, sweetener, and ½ cup chicken broth and set aside.

3. Bring the 3 cups chicken broth to a boil in a wok or skillet, then reduce to a simmer. Add the drained pieces of marinated chicken and cook not quite all the way through. Remove the chicken from the wok, drain, and keep warm.

4. Put the broccoli in the simmering chicken broth and cook until crisp-tender. Drain and arrange in a ring on a serving platter and keep warm. Discard the broth and wipe the wok clean.

5. Heat the wok again and add the margarine. Add the ginger, green onion, and garlic, sautéing for just a few seconds. Add the stir-fry sauce and simmer for a few minutes.

6. Add the reserved chicken and cook all the way through, 2 to 4 minutes. Mix the cornstarch with the water and add to the simmering wok. Stir in the sesame oil. When the sauce has thickened, pour the stir-fry into the center of the broccoli ring.

Serves 4

NUTRITIONAL INFORMATION (PER SERVING)

Calories:	230
Fat:	5.79 grams
Protein:	32.03 grams
Carbohydrates:	13.67 grams
Dietary Fiber:	2.60 grams

The original P.F. Chang's China Bistro version has 275 calories per serving. By using egg substitute, artificial sweetener, and diet margarine, you save 45 calories per serving.

P.F. CHANG'S CHINA BISTRO
Spicy Chicken

Sauce

2 tablespoons diet margarine

2 tablespoons chopped garlic

3 tablespoons chopped green onions

1 cup pineapple juice

2 tablespoons chili garlic paste

2 tablespoons white vinegar

4 packets Sweet'n Low (or your favorite reduced-calorie sugar substitute for cooking)

1 teaspoon soy sauce

2 tablespoons water

½ teaspoon cornstarch

1 tablespoon diet margarine

12 ounces boneless, skinless chicken breasts, cut into bite-sized pieces

⅓ cup cornstarch

1. To make the sauce, melt the margarine in a small saucepan and sauté the garlic and green onions just until the garlic is soft. Add the pineapple juice, chili garlic paste, vinegar, sweetener, and soy sauce. Bring to a boil.

2. Mix the water with the ½ teaspoon cornstarch and stir until smooth. Add to the sauce. Lower the heat to a simmer and let the sauce thicken, stirring occasionally. Set aside.

3. Melt the 1 tablespoon margarine in a wok or large skillet. Toss the chicken pieces with the ⅓ cup cornstarch and stir-fry until light brown. Remove the chicken pieces from the wok. Add the sauce to the wok and heat through. Return the chicken pieces to the wok and toss with the sauce.

4. Transfer to a serving platter.

Serves 4

Calories: 260
Fat: 4.12 grams
Protein: 6.54 grams
Carbohydrates: 22.63 grams
Dietary Fiber: 0.28 gram

The original P.F. Chang's China Bistro version has 323 calories per serving. By using diet margarine and artificial sweetener, you save 63 calories per serving.

P.F. CHANG'S CHINA BISTRO
Stir-Fried Spicy Eggplant

Spicy Sauce

2 tablespoons oyster sauce

2 tablespoons soy sauce

2 tablespoons water

1 tablespoon white vinegar

3 packets Truvia (or your favorite reduced-calorie sugar substitute for cooking)

1 teaspoon sambal oelek chili paste

½ teaspoon ground bean sauce

½ teaspoon sesame oil

1 pound eggplant, peeled and cut into 1-inch cubes

1 tablespoon diet margarine

1 teaspoon minced garlic

2 green onions, sliced

1 tablespoon cornstarch

2 tablespoons water

1. Make the spicy sauce by whisking together all the sauce ingredients. Set aside until ready to use.

2. Preheat the oven to 400°F.

3. Place the eggplant cubes on a baking sheet that has been sprayed with cooking spray. Bake for about 20 minutes, until thoroughly cooked.

4. Melt the margarine in a large skillet or wok. Stir-fry the garlic and green onions until the garlic is soft. Add the sauce and let the mixture simmer for 2 minutes.

5. Add the eggplant cubes to the sauce. Simmer for a few more minutes. Mix the cornstarch with the water and stir into the skillet. Let the sauce simmer until thickened. Transfer to a platter and serve.

Serves 4

Calories: 102
Fat: 1.98 grams
Protein: 1.26 grams
Carbohydrates: 9.19 grams
Dietary Fiber: 2.88 grams

The original P.F. Chang's China Bistro version has 270 calories per serving. By using a sugar substitute and diet margarine and baking the eggplant instead of frying, you save 168 calories per serving.

PLANET HOLLYWOOD
Cap'n Crunch Chicken

1½ cups Cap'n Crunch cereal, crushed
1 cup cornflakes, crushed
1 egg
1 cup skim milk
1 teaspoon onion powder
1 teaspoon garlic powder
½ teaspoon pepper
2 pounds boneless, skinless chicken breasts, cut into strips

1. Preheat the oven to 350°F.
2. Combine the cereals in a large bowl and set aside.
3. Beat the egg with the milk. Add the onion powder, garlic powder, and pepper to the egg mixture.
4. Dip each strip of chicken into the egg mixture, then dip each strip into the cereal mixture, coating well.
5. Place the coated chicken strips on a baking sheet sprayed with cooking spray.
6. Bake for about 20 minutes, until the chicken is cooked all the way through.

Serves 8

NUTRITIONAL INFORMATION (PER SERVING)
Calories: 187
Fat: 4.29 grams
Protein: 25.42 grams
Carbohydrates: 9.26 grams
Dietary Fiber: 0.29 gram

The original Planet Hollywood version has 240 calories per serving. By using a little less cereal to coat the chicken and baking instead of frying, you save 53 calories per serving.

RAINFOREST CAFE
Blue Mountain Grilled Chicken Sandwich

4 low-fat whole wheat hamburger buns
4 boneless, skinless chicken breasts
1 tablespoon Cajun seasoning
¼ cup teriyaki sauce

Dressing
¼ cup low-fat mayonnaise
2 tablespoons honey mustard

1 teaspoon curry powder
Dash of Tabasco sauce
8 lettuce leaves
4 slices cooked turkey bacon
4 slices low-fat Swiss cheese
One 7-ounce jar roasted red peppers, drained
1 cup coleslaw

1. Preheat the grill to medium heat.
2. Meanwhile, split and toast the hamburger buns, and rub the chicken with the Cajun seasoning.
3. Grill the chicken breasts until cooked through, then brush with the teriyaki sauce and set aside.
4. Mix the dressing ingredients together in a small bowl.
5. Using 1 tablespoon of the dressing per bun, spread the dressing on both sides of each bun.
6. Assemble each sandwich with 2 lettuce leaves, 1 slice of bacon, 1 slice of cheese, ¼ cup of the roasted red peppers, and a chicken breast.
7. Serve with ¼ cup coleslaw per sandwich.

Serves 4

NUTRITIONAL INFORMATION (PER SERVING)
Calories: 402
Fat: 13.18 grams
Protein: 43.16 grams
Carbohydrates: 39.32 grams
Dietary Fiber: 0.34 gram

The original Rainforest Cafe version has 875 calories per serving. By using turkey bacon and low-fat cheese and mayonnaise, and decreasing the amount of bacon, cheese, dressing, and coleslaw, you save 473 calories per serving.

RAINFOREST CAFE
Crab Cakes

Juice of ½ lemon
1 tablespoon Worcestershire
   sauce
¾ cup egg substitute (such as
   Egg Beaters)
½ teaspoon dry mustard
½ teaspoon black pepper
Pinch of red pepper flakes

Pinch of Old Bay Seasoning
Pinch of salt
2 tablespoons low-fat mayonnaise
4 slices Sara Lee diet wheat bread
¼ cup finely chopped fresh parsley
1 pound lump crabmeat
2 tablespoons diet margarine,
   melted

1. Mix together the lemon juice, Worcestershire sauce, egg substitute, mustard, black pepper, red pepper flakes, Old Bay Seasoning, salt, and mayonnaise in a large bowl.

2. Toast the bread until it is completely dry and crumble into crumbs.

3. Add the bread crumbs and parsley to the bowl and mix well.

4. Be sure the crabmeat has no bits of shell by picking through it carefully with your fingers. Add the crabmeat to the bread mixture and mix lightly.

5. Make into four 3-inch patties. Sauté the patties in the melted margarine for 2 to 3 minutes on each side, until brown.

Serves 4

NUTRITIONAL INFORMATION (PER SERVING)

Calories: 205
Fat: 7.07 grams
Protein: 26.50 grams
Carbohydrates: 6.89 grams
Dietary Fiber: 0.92 gram

The original Rainforest Cafe version has 465 calories per serving. By using egg substitute, low-fat mayonnaise, and diet margarine, and making your own bread crumbs with diet bread, you save 260 calories per serving.

RED LOBSTER
Clam Chowder

⅔ cup all-purpose flour
4 cups clam juice
1¾ cups chicken broth
1 cup skim milk
2 ribs celery, finely chopped
1 tablespoon onion flakes

One 10-ounce can clams, drained
Pinch of parsley flakes
2 medium baked potatoes, peeled
  and diced
Salt and pepper

1. Whisk the flour into 1 cup of the clam juice until well blended and there are no lumps. Add the remaining 3 cups clam juice, the chicken broth, and milk.

2. Simmer the mixture, stirring constantly, in a large saucepan over medium-high heat until thick and smooth.

3. Reduce the heat to low; stir in the celery, onion flakes, clams, parsley flakes, and diced potatoes.

4. Simmer for 15 to 20 minutes, until the potatoes are tender. Season with salt and pepper to taste.

Makes 4 servings

NUTRITIONAL INFORMATION (PER SERVING)
Calories: 275
Fat: 1.86 grams
Protein: 23.43 grams
Carbohydrates: 37.03 grams
Dietary Fiber: 2.92 grams

The original Red Lobster version has 480 calories per serving. By using skim milk and eliminating the extra heavy cream, you save 205 calories per serving.

RED LOBSTER
Shrimp Scampi

¼ cup white wine
¾ cup chicken broth
3 tablespoons minced garlic
1 pound medium shrimp, peeled and deveined

4 tablespoons (¼ cup) diet margarine
Salt and pepper
1 tablespoon chopped fresh parsley, for garnish

1. Heat a skillet and add the wine, broth, and garlic. Let the liquid reduce by half. The garlic should be soft.
2. Add the shrimp and stir until they are almost pink all the way through. Lower the heat.
3. Start whisking in the margarine, 1 tablespoon at a time, until it is all incorporated and the sauce is smooth. Season with salt and pepper and garnish with the parsley.

Serves 4

NUTRITIONAL INFORMATION (PER SERVING)

Calories:	145
Fat:	8.18 grams
Protein:	15.77 grams
Carbohydrates:	1.59 grams
Dietary Fiber:	0.18 gram

The original Red Lobster version has 180 calories per serving. By using chicken broth to replace some of the wine and using diet margarine, you save 35 calories per serving.

RED ROBIN
Banzai Burger

¼ cup teriyaki sauce
One 4-ounce extra-lean ground
  beef patty (95% lean)
1 canned pineapple ring (packed in
  juice, not syrup)
1 slice low-fat American cheese

1 low-fat whole wheat hamburger
  bun
1 tablespoon low-fat mayonnaise
¼ cup shredded lettuce
2 tomato slices

1. Pour the teriyaki sauce into a shallow bowl. Add the meat patty, turning to coat both sides. Refrigerate for 30 minutes.

2. Preheat the grill to medium heat.

3. Grill or sear the patty until cooked to the desired doneness, turning once. Remove the patty from the grill and keep warm.

4. Sear or broil the pineapple ring, turning once, until there is some charring on each side. Put the pineapple ring on the cooked patty and top with the cheese.

5. Toast the hamburger bun, then spread the top and bottom halves with the mayonnaise. Place the patty on the bottom half of the bun and top with the shredded lettuce and the tomato slices. Cover with the top half of the bun and serve.

Serves 1

NUTRITIONAL INFORMATION (PER SERVING)

Calories: 465
Fat: 12.93 grams
Protein: 37.01 grams
Carbohydrates: 55.20 grams
Dietary Fiber: 6.40 grams

The original Red Robin version has 1,033 calories per serving. By using very lean beef and a slightly smaller patty (4 ounces instead of 5 ounces), and using low-fat cheese, low-fat mayonnaise, and a low-fat whole wheat bun, you save 568 calories per serving.

RED ROBIN
BBQ Chicken Salad

Barbecue Sauce
½ cup tomato sauce
I teaspoon Worcestershire sauce
½ teaspoon liquid smoke
I teaspoon garlic powder
I teaspoon onion powder
I packet Sweet'n Low (or your favorite reduced-calorie sugar substitute for cooking)
I teaspoon yellow mustard

I boneless, skinless chicken breast
2 cups chopped romaine lettuce

2 cups chopped green-leaf or iceberg lettuce
½ cup chopped red cabbage
I small tomato, chopped
½ cup fat-free refried black beans
½ cup shredded low-fat Cheddar cheese
¼ avocado, sliced, for garnish
¼ cup fat-free ranch dressing, for serving

1. Preheat the grill to medium heat.

2. Make the barbecue sauce by whisking the ingredients together. (If you plan to use some of the barbecue sauce for serving with the salad, set it aside from the sauce that is used to coat the chicken.)

3. Place the chicken on the grill, brushing both sides generously with the barbecue sauce once the chicken is half cooked. Continue to brush with the sauce as the chicken grills.

4. Combine the lettuces and cabbage and arrange on a serving plate; top with the chopped tomato.

5. In a sauté pan, heat the beans. Spread the beans over the lettuce mixture on one side of the plate.

6. Slice the cooked chicken and spread it on the lettuce mixture opposite the beans.

7. Sprinkle the cheese over the top.

8. Garnish with the avocado slices and serve with the ranch dressing and the reserved barbecue sauce on the side.

Serves 1

Calories: 540
Fat: 14.78 grams
Protein: 51.17 grams
Carbohydrates: 54.27 grams
Dietary Fiber: 15.10 grams

The original Red Robin version has 1,095 calories per serving. By making your own barbecue sauce, using fat-free beans, low-fat cheese, and fat-free ranch dressing, and eliminating the crunchy onion rings, you save 555 calories per serving.

RED ROBIN
Burnin' Love Burger

Chipotle Mayonnaise

1 tablespoon fat-free mayonnaise

⅛ teaspoon chipotle chile powder

⅛ teaspoon paprika

6 ounces extra-lean ground beef (95% lean)

¼ teaspoon salt

⅛ teaspoon chili powder

⅛ teaspoon cumin

⅛ teaspoon black pepper

1 slice low-fat pepper Jack cheese

1 Wonder light hamburger bun, split in half

4 to 6 slices jalapeño pepper

2 tablespoons fresh salsa or pico de gallo (see page 11)

⅓ cup shredded iceberg lettuce

1. Prepare the chipotle mayonnaise by combining the ingredients in a small bowl. Mix well.

2. Preheat the grill to medium heat.

3. Shape the beef into a patty that is slightly larger than the bun. Season the meat on both sides with the salt, chili powder, cumin, and black pepper. Place the meat patty on the grill. Grill to the desired doneness. Just before the burger is done, place the cheese on top and allow it to melt.

4. Meanwhile, toast both sides of the bun and spread with the chipotle mayonnaise. Place the patty on the bottom half of the bun. Top with the jalapeño slices and the salsa. Place the shredded lettuce over the salsa and cover with the top half of the bun.

Serves 1

Calories: 390
Fat: 17.09 grams
Protein: 42.14 grams
Carbohydrates: 15.01 grams
Dietary Fiber: 2.59 grams

The original Red Robin version has 936 calories per serving. By using fat-free mayonnaise, very lean hamburger meat, 1 slice of low-fat cheese, and a low-fat bun, you save 546 calories per serving.

RUBY TUESDAY
Chicken Quesadillas

6 ounces boneless, skinless chicken breast
Salt and pepper
1 teaspoon onion powder
1 teaspoon garlic powder
Two 6-inch flour tortillas
2 tablespoons diet margarine, melted
½ cup shredded low-fat Monterey Jack or Cheddar cheese

1 tablespoon diced tomato
1 tablespoon diced jalapeño pepper
Cajun seasoning

To Serve
Shredded lettuce
Diced tomato
1 tablespoon fat-free sour cream
Salsa

1. Place the chicken in a bowl with salt and pepper, the onion powder, and the garlic powder. Be sure all the chicken is seasoned. Allow it to sit for 30 minutes in the refrigerator.

2. Preheat the grill to medium heat.

3. Grill the chicken for 10 to 12 minutes, until no longer pink. Cut into ¾-inch cubes and set aside.

4. Brush both sides of both tortillas with the melted margarine. Lightly brown one side of 1 tortilla in a skillet over medium heat and then remove it from the skillet.

5. Brown one side of the second tortilla, then flip that tortilla in the skillet.

6. Top the flipped tortilla with the cheese, tomato, jalapeño pepper, and Cajun seasoning. Spread these ingredients evenly and then top with the cubed chicken.

7. Place the browned side of the first tortilla on top of the chicken on the second tortilla. Allow to cook for about 1 minute, then turn the entire quesadilla to brown the remaining side.

8. Remove the quesadilla from the pan and cut into 6 wedges. Serve with shredded lettuce, diced tomato, sour cream, and salsa.

Makes 3 servings (2 wedges each)

Calories: 195
Fat: 9.02 grams
Protein: 18.13 grams
Carbohydrates: 10.99 grams
Dietary Fiber: 1.36 grams

The original Ruby Tuesday version has 294 calories per serving. By using 2 smaller tortillas, diet margarine, low-fat cheese, and fat-free sour cream, you save 99 calories per serving.

RUBY TUESDAY
Shrimp Pasta Parmesan

3 tablespoons diet margarine, melted
1 teaspoon dried oregano
½ teaspoon salt
Black pepper
16 large shrimp, peeled and deveined
1 pound cremini mushrooms, sliced
1 large onion, finely chopped
¼ teaspoon red pepper flakes
1 tablespoon chopped fresh thyme
1 large tomato, chopped
3 cloves garlic, minced
½ cup dry white wine
⅓ cup all-purpose flour
3 cups skim milk
1 cup chicken broth
⅛ teaspoon ground nutmeg
8 ounces pasta (penne, rigatoni, or fettuccine)
⅓ cup grated low-fat Parmigiano-Reggiano cheese

1. In a small bowl, mix together 1 tablespoon of the melted margarine, the oregano, the salt, and black pepper to taste. Brush the mixture over the shrimp.

2. Preheat a griddle on medium-high heat. Sear the shrimp on the griddle for about 2 minutes per side. Transfer to a medium bowl.

3. Pour 1 tablespoon of the melted margarine into a sauté pan. Add the mushrooms and sauté over medium-high heat until the liquid from the mushrooms evaporates.

4. Add the onion, red pepper flakes, and thyme and sauté until the onion is translucent, about 8 minutes.

5. Add the chopped tomato and garlic and sauté for 2 minutes, then add the wine and simmer for 2 minutes more, or until the liquid evaporates.

6. Transfer the mushroom-tomato mixture to the bowl with the shrimp.

7. Pour the remaining 1 tablespoon melted margarine into the same pan over medium-low heat. Using a wire whisk, add the flour and whisk for about 2 minutes, then whisk in the milk, broth, and nutmeg.

8. Increase the heat to high while stirring to prevent scorching. Once the mixture starts to boil, reduce the heat to low. Simmer, uncovered, whisking often, until the sauce thickens, about 15 minutes.

9. Meanwhile, cook the pasta until al dente. Drain and toss with the sauce. Remove the pasta and sauce from the stove top and add the shrimp mixture. Add the cheese and toss before serving.

Serves 4

NUTRITIONAL INFORMATION (PER SERVING)

Calories:	525
Fat:	6.41 grams
Protein:	26.36 grams
Carbohydrates:	74.63 grams
Dietary Fiber:	7.9 grams

The original Ruby Tuesday version has 1,050 calories per serving. By using diet margarine, skim milk, and low-fat cheese and decreasing the amount of pasta per serving, you cut the calories in half, saving 525 calories per serving.

RUBY TUESDAY
Sonoran Chicken Pasta

Sonoran Cheese Sauce

4 tablespoons (¼ cup) diet margarine

½ cup finely chopped onion

I small clove garlic, minced

I jalapeño pepper, seeded and minced

⅓ cup all-purpose flour

I cup hot water

I tablespoon chicken bouillon powder

I cup skim milk

½ teaspoon salt

I packet Sweet'n Low (or your favorite reduced-calorie sugar substitute for cooking)

¼ teaspoon Tabasco sauce

I teaspoon lemon juice

¼ teaspoon cayenne pepper

¾ cup shredded low-fat Parmesan cheese

½ can condensed Cheddar cheese soup (such as Campbell's), not diluted

¾ cup salsa

½ cup fat-free sour cream

8 ounces penne pasta, cooked until al dente

6 ounces boneless, skinless chicken breast, grilled and cut into ¼-inch-thick slices

⅓ cup canned black beans, drained and rinsed

¼ cup diced tomato

I teaspoon chopped green onion

1. To make the Sonoran cheese sauce, melt the margarine in a large saucepan and add the onion, garlic, and jalapeño.

2. Sauté until the onion is translucent.

3. Stir in the flour to make a roux and cook, stirring often, for 5 minutes.

4. Mix together the hot water, bouillon powder, and milk. Add the mixture slowly to the roux, stirring constantly.

5. Allow the sauce to cook for about 5 minutes. Add the salt, sweetener, Tabasco, lemon juice, cayenne, and Parmesan cheese. Stir to blend. Do not allow to boil. Add the cheese soup and stir until mixed well. Add the salsa and sour cream and stir to blend.

6. To assemble the pasta, place the cooked penne in a medium bowl. Add ¾ cup of the cheese sauce and toss to coat evenly. Pour into a large

serving bowl. Place the sliced chicken on top of the pasta, then ladle the black beans over the top. Sprinkle with the diced tomato and green onion.

Serves 4

NUTRITIONAL INFORMATION (PER SERVING)

Calories:	375
Fat:	28.34 grams
Protein:	26.01 grams
Carbohydrates:	67.12 grams
Dietary Fiber:	8.39 grams

The original Ruby Tuesday version has 865 calories per serving. By using diet margarine, skim milk, low-fat cheese, and fat-free sour cream, you save 490 calories per serving.

SBARRO
Baked Ziti

2 pounds whole wheat ziti pasta
2 pounds low-fat ricotta cheese
3 ounces grated low-fat Romano cheese
3 cups tomato sauce

1 tablespoon onion powder
1 teaspoon garlic powder
½ teaspoon pepper
1½ pounds low-fat mozzarella cheese, shredded

1. In a large pot of boiling salted water, cook the ziti for 12 to 14 minutes, until al dente, stirring often. When done, drain, but do not rinse.

2. Meanwhile, preheat the oven to 350°F.

3. In a large bowl, combine the ricotta, Romano, 2¾ cups of the tomato sauce, the onion powder, garlic powder, and pepper. Blend well. Add the cooked ziti to the mixture and stir well.

4. Spread the remaining ¼ cup tomato sauce on the bottom of a 13 by 9-inch baking pan.

5. Transfer the ziti to the baking pan and top with the mozzarella cheese. Cover loosely with foil.

6. Bake in the preheated oven until the cheese is melted and the ziti is heated through, 15 to 20 minutes.

Serves 6

NUTRITIONAL INFORMATION (PER SERVING)
Calories: 962
Fat: 17.04 grams
Protein: 79.70 grams
Carbohydrates: 132.51 grams
Dietary Fiber: 18.58 grams

The original Sbarro version has 1,273 calories per serving. By using whole wheat pasta and low-fat cheeses, you save 311 calories per serving. If you made 8 servings from this dish, there would be 722 calories per serving. Also, if you cut the amount of low-fat ricotta and mozzarella cheeses in half, you could have 6 servings at 780 calories each or 8 servings at 585 calories each.

SBARRO

Chicken Francese with Lemon Butter

1¼ cups egg substitute (such as Egg Beaters)
¼ cup grated low-fat Romano cheese
1 teaspoon parsley flakes
½ cup all-purpose flour
Five 5-ounce boneless, skinless chicken breasts, pounded ¼ inch thick

9 tablespoons diet margarine
½ cup sliced mushrooms
1 cup chicken broth
Juice of 2 lemons
Salt and white pepper
Chopped fresh parsley, for garnish
Lemon slices, for garnish

1. Preheat the oven to 350°F.

2. Pour the egg substitute into a bowl and stir in the cheese and parsley flakes. Place the flour in a shallow bowl. Dip the chicken in the egg mixture, then in the flour. Place on a baking sheet sprayed with cooking spray.

3. Bake the chicken for 25 to 30 minutes, until no longer pink.

4. Melt 1 tablespoon of the margarine in a skillet and add the mushrooms. Sauté the mushrooms over medium heat until browned. Remove from the pan and set aside.

5. Add the chicken broth to the skillet. Bring it to a boil and reduce by half. Add the lemon juice, then the remaining 8 tablespoons margarine, whisking constantly until it is melted. Return the mushrooms to the pan. Season with salt and white pepper.

6. Plate the chicken breasts and pour the sauce over the top. Garnish with parsley and lemon slices.

Serves 5

Calories: 345
Fat: 17.66 grams
Protein: 39.19 grams
Carbohydrates: 11.61 grams
Dietary Fiber: 0.40 gram

The original Sbarro version has 641 calories per serving. By using egg substitute, less flour, and diet margarine and baking instead of frying, you save 296 calories per serving.

SBARRO

Rigatoni alla Vodka

1 tablespoon diet margarine
2 cloves garlic, minced
One 24-ounce can tomato sauce
½ teaspoon whole pink
  peppercorns, cracked
1 tablespoon salt
½ teaspoon black pepper
1 teaspoon dried basil

1 cup skim milk
One 3-ounce package fat-free
  cream cheese, softened
3 tablespoons vodka
2 pounds rigatoni pasta, cooked
  until al dente
2 tablespoons chopped fresh
  parsley

1. Melt the margarine in a medium saucepan and sauté the garlic until translucent. Add the tomato sauce and the cracked pink peppercorns. Season with the salt and black pepper, then add the dried basil. Simmer for 10 minutes over low heat.

2. Whisk in the milk, cream cheese, and vodka. Simmer for 5 minutes, or until the sauce is slightly thickened.

3. Toss with the rigatoni and garnish with the parsley.

Serves 8

NUTRITIONAL INFORMATION (PER SERVING)

Calories: 488
Fat: 2.93 grams
Protein: 18.87 grams
Carbohydrates: 92.22 grams
Dietary Fiber: 4.93 grams

The original Sbarro version has 640 calories per serving. By using diet margarine instead of oil, and skim milk and fat-free cream cheese instead of heavy cream, you save 152 calories per serving.

SHONEY'S
Chicken Stir-Fry

6 ounces boneless, skinless chicken breast, cut into pieces
½ cup teriyaki sauce
½ cup white rice
3 tablespoons diet margarine
Salt and pepper
1 cup chicken broth
3 mushrooms, sliced
½ medium onion, cut into thin wedges
½ cup broccoli florets
½ cup shredded carrot
½ cup thinly sliced green bell pepper

1. Marinate the chicken pieces in ¼ cup of the teriyaki sauce for at least 2 hours in the refrigerator.

2. Place the rice in a saucepan with 1 tablespoon of the margarine and salt and pepper to taste. Cook, stirring, over medium heat, until the margarine is melted and the rice begins to slightly brown. Stir in the chicken broth. Cover the pan and reduce the heat to low. Cook for about 20 minutes.

3. Melt the remaining 2 tablespoons of the margarine in a skillet and sauté the chicken pieces until cooked through. Discard the marinade. Add the mushrooms and the remaining ¼ cup teriyaki sauce and stir-fry for 1 minute. Add the onion, broccoli, carrot, and bell pepper. Cover the skillet for a few minutes and lower the heat, simmering until the vegetables are tender.

4. Take the lid off the pan, and toss the ingredients together to complete the stir-fry.

5. Divide the rice between two serving dishes and top with the stir-fried chicken and vegetables.

Serves 2

Calories: 470
Fat: 13.97 grams
Protein: 43.57 grams
Carbohydrates: 58.98 grams
Dietary Fiber: 2.95 grams

The original Shoney's version has 1,200 calories per serving. By using diet margarine instead of oil, increasing the amount of vegetables, and making the recipe for 2 servings rather than just 1, you save 730 calories per serving. (This is still 3 ounces of meat per serving.)

SHONEY'S
Strawberry Pie

Crust

1 cup all-purpose flour

¼ teaspoon salt

8 tablespoons (½ cup) diet margarine

2 tablespoons ice water

½ cup sugar

6 packets Sweet'n Low (or your favorite reduced-calorie sugar substitute for cooking)

3 tablespoons cornstarch

One 12-ounce can Diet 7Up

Red food coloring

1 pint strawberries

½ cup Cool Whip Lite topping, for garnish

8 hulled strawberries, for garnish

1. In a medium bowl, mix the flour and salt; using a pastry cutter or two forks, cut in the margarine until the mixture resembles coarse meal. Add the water, 1 drop at a time, and continue cutting until the dough coheres. Shape into a ball. Cover and refrigerate for 1 hour.

2. Meanwhile, in a medium saucepan, combine the sugar, 5 packets of the sweetener, the cornstarch, and Diet 7Up; whisk well. Cook, stirring, over medium heat, until the mixture becomes thick. Let cool to room temperature. Add a few drops of red food coloring and mix well.

3. Preheat the oven to 350°F.

4. Remove the dough from the refrigerator and let sit for 15 minutes before rolling. Pat the dough into a circle and roll it to fit a 9-inch pie pan. Place in the pan and crimp the edges. Transfer the piecrust to the oven and bake for 4 to 5 minutes, until the edge is light brown. Remove from the oven and let cool completely.

5. Rinse, drain, and hull the strawberries. Cut into quarters or smaller pieces, depending on their size, and place in a large bowl. Sprinkle lightly with the remaining 1 packet sweetener. Stir gently and pour the strawberries into the cooled pie shell. Pour the Diet 7Up mixture over the strawberries. Allow the pie to set for 10 minutes, then refrigerate for at least 4 hours.

6. To serve, top with 1 tablespoon of Cool Whip per slice and place a fresh strawberry on top.

Serves 8

NUTRITIONAL INFORMATION (PER SERVING)

Calories:	195
Fat:	5.33 grams
Protein:	2.14 grams
Carbohydrates:	36.82 grams
Dietary Fiber:	2.71 grams

The original Shoney's version has 340 calories per serving. By using diet margarine, artificial sweetener for some of the sugar, Diet 7Up, and Cool Whip Lite, you save 145 calories per serving.

STEAK AND ALE
Bourbon Street Steak

1½ teaspoons diced onion
1 tablespoon bourbon
1 tablespoon beef bouillon powder
3 tablespoons soy sauce
1 tablespoon packed dark brown sugar

2 packets Truvia (or your favorite reduced-calorie sugar substitute for cooking)
3 tablespoons lemon juice
1 clove garlic, chopped
One 8-ounce New York strip steak

1. Combine all the ingredients together except the steak. Whisk until all the ingredients are incorporated. Pour this marinade into a container and add the steak. Cover the container and marinate the meat for 4 hours, turning every 30 minutes.

2. Preheat the grill to medium heat or preheat the broiler.

3. Remove the steak from the marinade and grill it to the desired doneness. Discard the marinade.

Serves 1

NUTRITIONAL INFORMATION (PER SERVING)

Calories:	609
Fat:	35.13 grams
Protein:	46.74 grams
Carbohydrates:	12.01 grams
Dietary Fiber:	0.22 gram

The original Steak and Ale version has 938 calories per serving. By using less bourbon and less sugar and using an 8-ounce steak rather than a 10-ounce steak, you save 329 calories per serving.

STEAK AND ALE
Hawaiian Chicken

¼ cup soy sauce
½ cup dry sherry
I cup unsweetened pineapple juice
¼ cup red wine vinegar
6 packets Truvia (or your favorite
reduced-calorie sugar substitute
for cooking)

½ teaspoon garlic powder
Six 5-ounce boneless, skinless
chicken breasts
½ cup shredded low-fat provolone
cheese

1. Combine the soy sauce, sherry, pineapple juice, vinegar, sweetener, and garlic powder for the marinade. Add the chicken, cover, and refrigerate overnight, turning occasionally.

2. Preheat the grill to medium heat or preheat the broiler. Remove the chicken from the marinade and place on the heated grill. Cook the chicken, turning once and basting each uncooked side, until cooked through. Discard the marinade.

3. Just before the chicken is done, sprinkle a small amount of cheese on each piece. Remove from the grill and serve.

Serves 6

NUTRITIONAL INFORMATION (PER SERVING)
Calories: 225
Fat: 5.39 grams
Protein: 33.59 grams
Carbohydrates: 6.27 grams
Dietary Fiber: 0.17 gram

The original Steak and Ale version has 319 calories per serving. By using a little less pineapple juice and a sugar substitute, you save 94 calories per serving.

TEXAS ROADHOUSE
Legendary Sirloin Beef Tips

Salt and pepper
Garlic powder
2 tablespoons all-purpose flour
3 tablespoons diet margarine
4 ounces sirloin steak, cut into
large cubes

1 small onion, diced
4 large mushrooms, sliced
¼ cup white wine
½ cup beef broth
1 tablespoon cornstarch
½ cup prepared whole grain rice

1. Mix salt and pepper and garlic powder together and stir into the flour. Melt 1 tablespoon of the margarine in a skillet. Dredge the steak pieces with the flour mixture, then sauté the meat until it is medium-rare. Add the onion and cook until it is softened.

2. Add the remaining 2 tablespoons margarine to the pan and then add the mushrooms. Cook until the mushrooms begin to color. Remove the meat, onion, and mushrooms to a platter and keep warm.

3. Deglaze the skillet with the wine, making sure to loosen any browned bits, and let it reduce a little. Add the beef broth and bring to a boil. Return the reserved meat and vegetables to the pan and simmer, covered, for about 1 hour, until the meat is tender.

4. Mix the cornstarch with about 2 tablespoons of cold water and stir until smooth. Add to the simmering broth. When the sauce is thickened, serve with the beef tips over the rice.

Serves 1

NUTRITIONAL INFORMATION (PER SERVING)

Calories:	610
Fat:	38.02 grams
Protein:	29.64 grams
Carbohydrates:	48.35 grams
Dietary Fiber:	2.90 grams

The original Texas Roadhouse version has 1,053 calories per serving. By using diet margarine instead of olive oil, and decreasing the meat from 6 ounces to 4 ounces and the rice from 1 cup to ½ cup, you save 443 calories per serving.

TEXAS ROADHOUSE
Texas Steak Rolls

Barbecue Sauce
2½ cups tomato sauce
2 tablespoons dark brown sugar
2 tablespoons yellow mustard
2 tablespoons Worcestershire
sauce
1 tablespoon garlic powder
1 tablespoon onion powder
1 teaspoon red pepper flakes

Dipping Sauce
3 cups fat-free mayonnaise
1 cup Barbecue Sauce (above)
1 tablespoon black pepper
1 tablespoon white pepper

Texas Rolls
2 pounds grilled or broiled sirloin
steak, cut into ½-inch cubes
8 ounces low-fat Cheddar cheese,
shredded
1 medium onion, cut into ¼-inch
cubes
2 jalapeño peppers, minced
1½ cups Barbecue Sauce (above)
1 large egg, beaten
24 egg roll wrappers (7 inches
square)
2 tablespoons diet margarine,
melted

1. Begin by making the barbecue sauce. Mix all the ingredients together with a whisk. Set aside until ready to use.

2. Make the dipping sauce. Whisk all the ingredients together and refrigerate until ready to serve.

3. Combine the steak pieces, cheese, onion, and jalapeños. Add the 1½ cups barbecue sauce; mix well.

4. Whisk together the egg and ½ cup of water to make an egg wash.

5. Fill each wrapper with ⅓ cup of the meat mixture, following the directions on the wrapper package. Seal the corners of the wrapper with the egg wash, pressing firmly to make sure they stick. Refrigerate the filled wrappers for 30 minutes.

6. Preheat the oven to 350°F.

7. Brush both sides of each filled wrapper with the melted margarine. Place the wrappers on a baking sheet that has been sprayed with cooking spray. Bake for 18 to 20 minutes, until the steak rolls are golden brown.

8. Serve with the dipping sauce.

Serves 6

NUTRITIONAL INFORMATION (PER SERVING)
Calories: 960
Fat: 34.71 grams
Protein: 28.60 grams
Carbohydrates: 94.88 grams
Dietary Fiber: 6.20 grams

The original Texas Roadhouse version has 3,540 calories per serving. By making your own barbecue sauce, using fat-free mayonnaise and low-fat cheese, baking instead of frying, and dividing the recipe into 6 servings instead of 4, you save 2,580 calories per serving. Even if you used this recipe to serve 4, you would still save 2,100 calories per serving.

T.G.I. FRIDAY'S
Au Gratin Potatoes

4 large baking potatoes, scrubbed

Béchamel Sauce

4 tablespoons (¼ cup) diet
  margarine

¼ cup all-purpose flour

2 cups skim milk

1 cup chicken broth

1 teaspoon salt

¼ teaspoon ground nutmeg

1 teaspoon salt

¼ teaspoon white pepper

½ cup grated low-fat mozzarella
  cheese

¼ cup grated low-fat Colby cheese

1. Bake the potatoes in advance in a 400°F oven until tender, about 1 hour. Let cool long enough to be able to make neat slices, about 30 minutes. Then slice into ½-inch-thick rounds.

2. To make the sauce, melt the margarine in a saucepan and whisk in the flour, stirring constantly, until the paste is smooth and a very light brown. Gradually add the milk and chicken broth, whisking, and season with the salt and nutmeg. Lower the heat and simmer for 15 minutes, or until the sauce thickens.

3. Preheat the oven to 300°F.

4. Put the sliced potatoes in a large bowl and season with the salt and white pepper. Add the cheeses, then fold in the warm béchamel sauce. Transfer the mixture to a 13 by 9-inch baking dish and cover with foil.

5. Bake until the cheeses melt, then remove the foil and allow the top to get bubbly and brown. Serve hot.

Serves 4

Calories: 285
Fat: 4.91 grams
Protein: 17.37 grams
Carbohydrates: 51.16 grams
Dietary Fiber: 4.93 grams

The original T.G.I. Friday's version has 345 calories per serving. By using diet margarine, skim milk, and low-fat cheeses, you save 60 calories per serving.

T.G.I. FRIDAY'S
Broccoli-Cheese Soup

4 cups water
2 cups diced peeled potatoes
2 chicken bouillon cubes
1 cup diced onion
Two 10-ounce packages frozen
  chopped broccoli

Two 10.75-ounce cans condensed
  cream of chicken soup
  (such as Campbell's)
Two 10.75-ounce cans condensed
  Cheddar cheese soup
  (such as Campbell's)

1. Combine the water, potatoes, bouillon cubes, onion, and broccoli in a large, heavy saucepan. Cook over medium heat for 20 minutes, or until the potatoes and broccoli are tender.

2. Add the canned soups, stirring until the soup is smooth. Simmer for 15 minutes, or until the soup thickens.

Serves 4

NUTRITIONAL INFORMATION (PER SERVING)

Calories: 308
Fat: 9.05 grams
Protein: 10.03 grams
Carbohydrates: 48.54 grams
Dietary Fiber: 7.11 grams

The original T.G.I. Friday's version has 527 calories per serving. By using Cheddar cheese soup instead of Velveeta, you save 219 calories per serving.

T.G.I. FRIDAY'S
Bruschetta Chicken

Balsamic Glaze

½ cup balsamic vinegar

3 packets Truvia (or your favorite reduced-calorie sweetener for cooking)

Garlic Butter

4 tablespoons (¼ cup) diet margarine, softened

½ teaspoon garlic powder

Salt and pepper

Marinated Tomatoes

5 fresh basil leaves, shredded

6 large Roma tomatoes, diced

2 cloves garlic, minced

1 teaspoon ground oregano

1 teaspoon onion powder

Bruschetta Marinara Sauce

2 cloves garlic, sliced

¼ teaspoon salt

⅛ teaspoon pepper

½ cup tomato sauce

5 fresh basil leaves, shredded

4 slices Sara Lee diet wheat bread

Chicken and Pasta

4 boneless, skinless chicken breasts

Salt and pepper

12 ounces angel hair pasta, cooked until al dente

2 tablespoons grated low-fat Parmesan cheese

1. Make the balsamic glaze in a small saucepan. Simmer the vinegar and sweetener until the liquid is reduced to ¼ cup.

2. Combine the softened margarine, garlic powder, and salt and pepper to taste to make the garlic butter.

3. To marinate the tomatoes, add the shredded basil to the diced tomatoes. Toss with the garlic, oregano, and onion powder. Set aside until needed.

4. To make the marinara sauce, sauté the garlic in 2 tablespoons of the garlic butter until the garlic softens. Add the salt, pepper, tomato sauce, and shredded basil. Simmer for about 5 minutes. Take the pan off the heat and set aside.

5. Preheat the broiler.

6. Spread the remaining 2 tablespoons garlic butter on the 4 slices of wheat bread. Toast under the broiler until a light golden brown.

7. Season the chicken with salt and pepper. Broil, turning once, until cooked through and no longer pink in the middle. Slice each breast into 4 strips.

8. Combine the marinated tomatoes with the marinara sauce. Toss the angel hair pasta with the mixture and divide among four plates. Layer the chicken strips over the pasta. Sprinkle each dish with the cheese, then drizzle the balsamic glaze on top. Serve with the toasted garlic bread.

Serves 4

NUTRITIONAL INFORMATION (PER SERVING)

Calories:	655
Fat:	13.79 grams
Protein:	45.81 grams
Carbohydrates:	84.65 grams
Dietary Fiber:	9.33 grams

The original T.G.I. Friday's version has 1,172 calories per serving. By using diet margarine instead of butter and olive oil, diet bread, low-fat cheese, and 3 ounces instead of 4 ounces of pasta per serving, you save 517 calories per serving.

T.G.I. FRIDAY'S
Lemon Chicken Scaloppini

Lemon Cream Sauce
½ cup medium-dry white wine
½ cup chicken broth
2 tablespoons lemon juice
1 tablespoon diet margarine
½ cup skim milk
One 3-ounce package low-fat
  cream cheese, softened
½ teaspoon dried thyme
Salt and pepper

Chicken
2 tablespoons diet margarine
1 boneless, skinless chicken breast,
  pounded ¼ inch thick

1 cup sliced mushrooms
Juice of 1 lemon
¼ cup skim milk
½ canned artichoke, halved and
  split lengthwise
1 teaspoon minced fresh parsley

2 ounces angel hair pasta, cooked
  until al dente
1 tablespoon drained capers

1. To make the lemon cream sauce, combine the wine, chicken broth, and lemon juice and boil until reduced to ¼ cup. Lower the heat and whisk in the margarine. Add the milk. Whisk in all of the cream cheese except 1 tablespoon. (Save for another use.) Season with the thyme and salt and pepper, and set aside.

2. Melt the margarine in a skillet and sauté the chicken, turning once, until it is cooked through and no longer pink in the middle. Add the sliced mushrooms and sauté until they absorb some of the liquid. Add the lemon juice and stir to blend. Add the milk and stir well.

3. Add the lemon cream sauce and the artichoke to the skillet, simmering for a few minutes. Add the parsley and stir.

4. Mound the cooked pasta in a warmed bowl and top with the chicken breast. Pour the mushroom–lemon cream sauce over the chicken and the pasta. Garnish with the capers.

Serves 1

Calories: 903
Fat: 29.99 grams
Protein: 84.75 grams
Carbohydrates: 74.53 grams
Dietary Fiber: 9.30 grams

The original T.G.I. Friday's version has 1,185 calories per serving. By replacing some of the wine with chicken broth, using diet margarine instead of butter and olive oil, replacing the heavy cream with fat-free cream cheese, and using a slightly smaller amount of pasta, you save 282 calories per serving.

UNION PACIFIC
Apple Pancakes

1 cup whole wheat flour	½ teaspoon vanilla extract
¼ teaspoon salt	2 packets Sweet'n Low (or your
1½ teaspoons baking powder	favorite reduced-calorie sugar
1 tablespoon diet margarine,	substitute for cooking)
melted	1¼ cups unsweetened applesauce
½ cup skim milk	
¼ cup egg substitute (such as	
Egg Beaters)	

1. Sift together the flour, salt, and baking powder into a medium bowl.
2. Combine the melted margarine, milk, and egg substitute. Stir into the flour mixture.
3. Add the vanilla, sweetener, and applesauce. Beat well.
4. Spoon the batter onto a hot griddle that has been sprayed with cooking spray. Use enough batter to make 4-inch pancakes. When the edges are slightly browned, turn the pancakes and cook on the other side.

Serves 2

NUTRITIONAL INFORMATION (PER SERVING)

Calories:	325
Fat:	5.25 grams
Protein:	12.81 grams
Carbohydrates:	63.18 grams
Dietary Fiber:	4.05 grams

The original Union Pacific version has 465 calories per serving. By using whole wheat flour, diet margarine, skim milk, egg substitute, and unsweetened applesauce, you save 140 calories per serving.

UNION PACIFIC
Grilled White Pekin Duck Breast

4 navel oranges
I tablespoon diet margarine, melted
I tablespoon soy sauce
2 tablespoons minced fresh mint
2 packets Sweet'n Low (or your favorite reduced-calorie sugar substitute for cooking)
I medium red onion, sliced into thin rings

Salt and pepper
4 boneless, skinless Pekin duckling breasts
I cup green seedless grapes
I head escarole, cored and chopped into I-inch pieces
6 ounces baby red romaine leaves

1. Juice 3 of the oranges.

2. Combine the orange juice with the melted margarine, soy sauce, mint, sweetener, and red onion. Mix well. Season with salt and pepper.

3. Marinate the duck breasts in half of this mixture for about 30 minutes. Remove the duck and discard the used marinade.

4. In a small saucepan, boil the remaining marinade for 1 minute. Set aside and let cool.

5. Peel the remaining orange and segment the pieces, removing any pith. Place the segments in a bowl with the grapes.

6. Preheat the grill to medium heat.

7. Pat the duck breasts dry; season on both sides with salt and pepper.

8. Place the duck breasts on the grill and cook for about 8 minutes for medium doneness. Remove from the grill and keep warm.

9. In a large bowl, lightly toss the chopped escarole and the romaine leaves with half of the reserved marinade.

10. Divide the greens equally among four plates.

11. Slice the duck breasts on an angle and place on top of the salad. Scatter the orange segments and grapes over each plateful.

12. Drizzle the remaining marinade over the top of each serving.

Serves 4

NUTRITIONAL INFORMATION (PER SERVING)
Calories: 280
Fat: 4.69 grams
Protein: 30.15 grams
Carbohydrates: 32.39 grams
Dietary Fiber: 1.75 grams

The original Union Pacific version has 345 calories per serving. By using diet margarine instead of sesame and grapeseed oils, you save 65 calories per serving.

UNO CHICAGO GRILL
Classic Deep-Dish Pizza

Dough

2¼ teaspoons (1 envelope)
active dry yeast
1 cup warm water (110° to
115°F)
3½ cups all-purpose flour
½ cup coarsely ground
cornmeal
1 teaspoon salt
⅛ cup vegetable oil

Pizza Topping

1 pound Italian sausage, removed
from the casings
One 15-ounce can whole tomatoes
8 ounces low-fat mozzarella
cheese, thinly sliced
2 cloves garlic, minced
5 fresh basil leaves, finely chopped
¼ cup grated low-fat Romano
cheese

1. In a large bowl, proof the yeast in the warm water until it foams, about 5 minutes. Add 1 cup of the flour, the cornmeal, salt, and vegetable oil. Stir to combine everything.

2. Continue adding the flour ½ cup at a time, stirring well after each addition, until the flour is used up. The dough should form a soft ball and come away from the sides of the bowl.

3. Lightly flour a work surface and begin to knead the dough until it reaches elasticity and is no longer very sticky, 10 to 12 minutes. Put the ball of dough in a lightly greased bowl, turning once to grease all sides, and cover with a damp dish towel. Set the bowl in an area free of drafts. Let the dough rise until doubled in size, about 1 hour.

4. Punch the dough down and briefly knead on a floured surface, about 2 minutes. Press the dough into a 15-inch deep-dish pizza pan that has been sprayed with cooking spray. Press it until it comes up about 2 inches on the sides of the pan and is even on the bottom. Cover and let rise for about 20 minutes.

5. To prepare the topping, sauté the sausage until it is cooked through, crumbling it as it cooks. Drain off the fat. Drain the tomatoes and coarsely chop them.

6. Preheat the oven to 500°F.

7. When the dough has completed the second rising, layer the sliced mozzarella over the bottom of the dough, followed by the sausage and then the garlic. Finish with the chopped tomatoes, basil, and Romano cheese.

8. Bake for 15 minutes at 500°F, then turn down the oven temperature to 400°F and bake for another 25 to 35 minutes. The crust should be a dark golden brown and slightly crispy. Cut into 8 slices and serve hot.

Serves 8

NUTRITIONAL INFORMATION (PER SERVING)

Calories:	430
Fat:	15.54 grams
Protein:	20.23 grams
Carbohydrates:	51.31 grams
Dietary Fiber:	2.80 grams

The original Uno Chicago Grill version has 770 calories per serving. By using low-fat cheeses, you save 340 calories per serving.

WHITE BARN INN RESTAURANT
Warm Chocolate Cake with Warm Chocolate Sauce

1 ½ cups egg substitute (such as
Egg Beaters)
⅓ cup sugar
8 ounces semisweet chocolate
4 tablespoons (¼ cup) diet
margarine
⅓ cup all-purpose flour, sifted
¾ cup skim milk

½ cup water
¼ cup sugar
4 packets Truvia (or your favorite
reduced-calorie sweetener for
cooking)
1 cup unsweetened cocoa
2 ounces semisweet chocolate
1 cup Cool Whip Lite topping

1. Preheat the oven to 375°F.

2. Spray 8 ramekins with cooking spray.

3. Beat the egg substitute and sugar together.

4. Melt the chocolate and margarine together and let cool.

5. Beat the chocolate-margarine mixture into the egg-sugar mixture. Fold in the flour. Spoon the batter into the prepared ramekins, dividing equally.

6. Bake the cakes for 10 minutes, or until the cakes feel firm at the edges. Let sit for about 5 minutes to cool, then unmold onto warmed serving plates.

7. In a heavy saucepan, heat the milk, water, sugar, sweetener, cocoa, and chocolate together over medium-low heat. Whisk frequently. As soon as the chocolate melts and the mixture comes to a boil, it is ready to serve. Remove from the heat.

8. Spoon the sauce over each cake. Top with a heaping teaspoonful of the whipped topping.

Serves 8

Recipe adapted from The White Barn Inn Cookbook: Four Seasons at the Celebrated American Inn, *by Jonathan Cartwright with Susan Sully (Philadelphia: Running Press Publishers, 2003).*

NUTRITIONAL INFORMATION (PER SERVING)

Calories:	318
Fat:	16.90 grams
Protein:	9.89 grams
Carbohydrates:	44.91 grams
Dietary Fiber:	5.79 grams

The original White Barn Inn version has 935 calories per serving. By using egg substitute, less sugar and chocolate, and diet margarine, and garnishing with low-fat whipped topping instead of vanilla bean ice cream, you save 617 calories per serving.

HEALTH AND NUTRITION GUIDE

Eating a Balanced Diet: What Does It Mean?

It's safe to say that we all want to eat better. Whether we want to slim down or just improve our overall energy and vitality, sticking to a healthy diet seems to be on everyone's mind these days. And many of us have concerns and questions about what we are eating and what we should be eating.

"Are carbs good or bad?" "Is a vegetarian diet best?" "Should I take vitamin supplements to make sure I am getting everything I need?"

To many, the components of a healthy and balanced diet seem confusing, even daunting. Given the enormous amount of diet and nutrition information available (at last check, Amazon.com listed over 100,000 books on the topic), many people aren't quite sure what it takes to develop good eating habits. However, once armed with a little basic information, we can begin to make wiser and healthier choices when it comes to the foods we eat.

First, it helps to keep a few basic principles in mind:

- Eat a wide variety of foods. The more types of foods you eat, the greater your chances of getting a balance of all the different nutrients you need. On the other hand, the more restricted your diet is, the less likely it is to give you all the nutrients you need.
- Eat fruits and vegetables with the brightest colors. Color is a tip-off that a fruit or vegetable contains the highest amounts of vitamins and antioxidants (more on those later).
- Make small changes in your diet over time; that way, you'll be more likely to stick with them. For example, you could start by

switching from whole to 2% or 1% milk. Give yourself a week or two to get used to it and then make the next change, such as adding a daily serving of fruit. Remember, it is not realistic to try to change your entire diet overnight.

- Eat a little bit less every day. Unless you are underweight (and most of us are not), it's a good practice. Eating even 100 fewer calories a day (about 1 tablespoon of butter or 1 slice of bread) can help you drop 10 pounds a year.
- Cook more meals at home. As was mentioned previously (see page xxiii), this can have a big effect on your weight and overall health.

The Basics: Carbohydrates, Protein, and Fat

Carbohydrates, protein, and fat are the three main building blocks of the foods that we eat. They all perform different and important functions in our bodies, and the amounts and types that we consume have a tremendous effect on our health.

Carbohydrates

Carbohydrates (often referred to as "carb" or "carbs") are the best fuel for the body, since they are easily burned for energy. In addition, carbohydrates form the bulk of what people in the United States eat—about 50 percent or more of our diet. Because of this, it's important to choose wisely from the wide variety of carbohydrate foods available to us.

Not all carbohydrates are created equal. "Complex carbohydrates," sometimes called "starches," are found in breads, crackers, cereals, pasta, rice, and potatoes, while "simple carbohydrates," also known as sugars, include table sugar (sucrose), sugar in fruit (fructose), honey, jam, and syrups.

Choosing the best kinds of carbohydrate foods used to be a black-and-white matter—complex carbs were thought to be good, because they are burned more slowly, while simple carbs were to be avoided, because they are quickly digested and therefore not as filling as complex carbs. We now know that the truth lies somewhere in the middle, since not all complex carbs are good for us and not all simple sugars need to be cut out.

In order to choose the best types of carbs, we need to know a little more about how they are handled by the body.

Complex carbs are either "whole grain" or "refined." Because whole grain carbs are not processed, they contain all the good things nature gave them—vitamins, minerals, fiber, antioxidants, and more. Many studies have shown that eating more whole grain foods helps lower blood sugar and cholesterol, improves digestion, and may help control weight. Examples of whole grains include brown rice; "regular" (not quick-cooking) oatmeal; whole wheat pasta, crackers, and breads; and cereals labeled "whole grain."

On the other hand, refined carbohydrates (white bread, white rice and pasta, and many popular breakfast cereals) go through lots of processing, including husking, grinding, and bleaching, which can destroy 50 percent or more of their nutritional value. Eating too many refined carbs has been linked with obesity and a greater chance of developing serious diseases, such as diabetes, cancer, and heart disease.

What about that simple carb sugar? We all know that America has a serious sweet tooth. From the jumbo-sized Coke bottles in our refrigerators to the breakfast cereal in our bowls, sugar seems to be in almost every food we eat. Here are just some of the names sugar has on food labels: sucrose, dextrose, maltose, fructose, agave nectar, invert sugar, cane juice, molasses, maltodextrin, and malt syrup.

Lately there has been a lot of coverage in the news about a sweetener called "high-fructose corn syrup," which is used as a replacement for sugar in many baked goods, beverages, and packaged snack foods. Some experts believe that eating a lot of foods with high-fructose corn syrup is linked with obesity, but there is no concrete proof of this. It's important to note that no one type of sugar is bad. The truth of the matter is that most of us simply eat too much sugar of *all* types, so the key is to try to cut down on the biggest sources—things like regular soda and candy, as well as the sugar we add to our coffee, tea, and cereal. And remember, sugar isn't necessarily bad for us. While it's true that eating too much sugar contributes to weight gain, sugar also provides us with energy that keeps our bodies running. So it is not desirable or even possible to cut out all sugars. We simply need to be choosy about where and how we get them—more from dairy products, fruits, and vegetables, and less from sweets and baked goods.

How many carbohydrates should we be eating? There is no one simple answer to this question. People who are physically active can eat more; those who are overweight or sedentary should eat less. Again, it is important to stress that carbs should not be eliminated from anyone's diet. Instead, it is important to watch the portion sizes and to emphasize whole grain choices.

Here are some typical portion sizes for carb foods:

- 1 slice of bread
- ½ English muffin or roll
- ½ cup rice, pasta, or noodles
- ½–1 cup cold cereal
- ½ cup oatmeal
- 1 small white or sweet potato

Best Complex Carb Choices: Whole grain breads, crackers, and cereals; brown rice; oatmeal; barley; and unusual grains like quinoa, bulgur, and buckwheat.

Best Sugar Choices: Natural sources like grapes, strawberries, oranges, and melons are surprisingly good for tackling a sweet tooth.

Protein

In recent years, various high-protein diets have been touted as healthy and effective ways to lose weight. From the Atkins diet revolution and the South Beach Diet to Protein Power, these plans promise weight loss through diets based on high amounts of protein foods and minimal amounts of carbohydrates. But do these high-protein diets work? In order to answer this question, it's important to understand what protein is and what it does in the body.

There are many types of proteins in nature. The proteins in our bodies perform highly specialized jobs. Some make up the structure of hair, skin, nails, tissues, and organs, while others form the complex enzymes and hormones that regulate virtually all of our bodily functions, from breathing and digestion to the mysterious and intricate workings of our brains.

Proteins vary in size and are formed by chains of smaller building blocks called amino acids. There are about twenty amino acids that exist widely across nature; of these, nine are called essential, because the body cannot make them, and they must be obtained from foods. Proteins from animal sources—meats, fish, poultry, eggs, and dairy products—are known as complete proteins, because they contain all of the essential amino acids. Proteins that come from plant and vegetable foods, such as nuts, legumes, beans, and grains, are known as incomplete proteins and need to be combined with other protein foods, in order to get a balance of essential amino acids.

How much protein do our bodies need? You might be surprised to learn that most of us require modest amounts to stay fit and healthy—roughly 50 grams per day for women and about 65 grams for men. Translated into food, 50 grams of protein looks something like this:

- 1 egg (6 grams)
- 1 cup yogurt or milk (8 grams)
- 3 ounces broiled chicken (25 grams)
- 1 slice of bread with 2 tablespoons peanut butter (12 grams)

Of course, there are exceptions to this "50/65"-gram guideline. Pregnant and nursing women and individuals who are ill or recovering from surgery or another physical trauma require greater amounts of protein, depending on age and overall health status. In addition, "extreme" athletes—those engaged in demanding sports and physical activities such as marathons and intensive weight training—may need extra protein to help rebuild muscle, in some cases as much as double the amount of protein needed by most people. It should be noted that some athletes choose to boost their dietary protein with supplements. However, such supplements are costly and unnecessary, and most athletes can adequately increase their protein intake by eating larger portions of high-quality protein foods.

So what about high-protein diets for weight loss? It's important to recognize that high-protein diets vary quite a bit in their approach.

Some severely restrict all types of carbohydrates, while others allow small amounts of carbohydrate foods that are complemented with larger portions of high-protein foods. Remember, the more restricted a diet is, the less healthy it is likely to be. This is particularly true for the strictest high-protein diets that don't allow much more than pure protein foods such as meat and eggs. These plans can also have negative effects on health. They may upset the body's calcium balance, leading to weakened bones, and may also stress the kidneys and other organs. In addition, they tend to be low in fiber, vitamins, and minerals.

Do high-protein diets work for weight loss? The answer is yes—in the short term. Because protein takes longer to digest than carbohydrates, it helps to give a feeling of fullness and decrease appetite. However, most people are just not able to stick to high-protein diets for more than a few weeks, because these diets are too limited to be satisfying over time. Once a person is off the diet and back to the normal routine, weight loss stops and weight gain begins. So, like all other weight-loss plans, high-protein diets do not provide a magic bullet for keeping the pounds off.

Best Protein Choices: Lean beef; skinless poultry; any type of fish, beans, and nuts; and eggs. (Yes, eggs; they really don't raise cholesterol as much as we once thought and are very high-quality protein. So eating 2 to 3 eggs a week is fine.)

Fat

Fat is needed by the body to perform many functions. It protects body organs, acts as an insulator, and is a storage site for vitamins A, D, E, and K (known as "fat-soluble" vitamins). Fat can also be burned for energy as needed.

It is no exaggeration to say that Americans have a love affair with high-fat food. From puffy éclairs billowing with whipped cream to pizza piled high with cheese, fat is a culinary goddess that adds flavor, body, and savory satisfaction to many of the foods we eat.

At the same time, the fat in our diet has been demonized, blamed for everything from obesity to heart disease and cancer. Until recently, *all* fats were thought to be bad, leading to recommendations to cut down on all types and amounts. But now we know that just like carbohydrates, not all fats are created equal. Some kinds of fats have good effects on our health and well-being, while other types are definite troublemakers. So whereas older dietary guidelines focused on cutting down on all kinds of fats, the most recent ones recommend replacing bad fats with good ones and worrying less about the total amount. In order to understand why some fats are better than others, a basic chemistry lesson outlining their differences is helpful.

Who's Who: Saturated vs. Unsaturated

All fats, also known as fatty acids, are formed by chains of carbon atoms that are linked together by bonds. If the carbon chain has no double bonds in it, the fatty acid is known as a saturated fat. Because they contain no double bonds, saturated fats are generally shaped like a straight chain and tend to be solid at room temperature. Saturated fats include many animal fats, such as butter and lard, and some vegetable fats, such as coconut, palm, and palm kernel oils.

Fatty acids containing one or more double bonds in their carbon chains are known as unsaturated fats; as a result of the double bonds, they tend to have a curved or "bent" shape. Unsaturated fats tend to be liquid at room temperature, like most vegetable oils. If there is one double bond in the carbon chain, the fat is called monounsaturated, and if there are two or more double bonds, the fat is termed polyunsaturated. As we shall see, these subtle variations in the way the carbon atoms of fatty acids are joined together account for huge differences in their effects on health.

The Good Guys: Mono- and Polyunsaturated Fats

Monounsaturated and polyunsaturated fats are two types of fats that we now know are very good for us—good for our hearts, our brains, and maybe even our waistlines. What are these good fats, and where are they found?

Some of the most important beneficial health effects linked to monounsaturated fat (MUFA) are that it helps to lower levels of bad (LDL) cholesterol and raise levels of good (HDL) cholesterol in the blood, seems to protect against diabetes and some types of cancers, may promote weight loss, and may even protect against Alzheimer's disease. A lot of the evidence for these good effects of MUFA comes from studies that have looked at the diets of people living in southern Italy and Greece. About twenty years ago, nutrition researchers began to notice that people who followed this so-called Mediterranean diet—lots of fruits and vegetables, limited meat and limited high-fat dairy foods, and liberal use of olives and olive oil in cooking—had very low rates of heart disease and cancer, even though they ate large amounts of fat. In time, the researchers concluded that the high content of MUFA in the Mediterranean diet was responsible for these fantastic benefits.

The Mediterranean diet is now widely promoted as being a sound, delicious, and healthy way to eat. In addition to being found in olives and olive oil, monounsaturated fat is found in large amounts in avocados, nuts (especially almonds and cashews), and canola oil.

Polyunsaturated fat (PUFA), found in safflower, sunflower, corn, and soybean oils, is another type of unsaturated fat that also offers several important health benefits. Like MUFA, polyunsaturated fat lowers levels of bad LDL cholesterol and helps raise levels of good HDL cholesterol in the blood. One unique kind of PUFA, known as omega-3, has been found to dramatically lower the risk of heart disease. It does this by reducing the dangerous inflammation that often leads to blocked arteries, and also by regulating blood clotting and preventing potentially dangerous heart arrhythmias. Omega-3 polyunsaturated fat is found mostly in flaxseed, walnuts, fish, and fish oil and is added to some so-called heart smart margarine-type spreads that are now on the market.

The Bad Guys: Saturated and Trans Fats

These two types of fats are truly the guys in the black hats, since nothing good can be said for either one. Both saturated and trans fats have earned their decidedly bad reputations for wrecking health and contributing to heart disease. Why are they so bad for us?

The answer is simple: Eating foods that contain either one (or both) dramatically increases our chances of developing heart disease. These fats do this by raising the levels of bad LDL cholesterol and lowering the amount of beneficial HDL cholesterol in our blood. It was once believed that saturated fat was the worst offender; we now know that trans fats are just as damaging (and may be more so) to our heart health.

So where are these dietary demons found, and how can we avoid them?

Saturated fat is found in regular dairy products (whole milk, "full-fat" cheeses, butter), red meat, coconut and coconut oil, and palm oil and palm kernel oil (which are now used in many prepared foods). The best way to cut down on saturated fat is to use low-fat/skim dairy products and to limit the amount of red meat we eat. We can also check labels on packaged and prepared foods like breakfast cereals, snacks, and baked goods and avoid those that contain palm and palm kernel oils.

Trans fats are a whole different animal. For the most part, they are not found in nature, but are instead formed by a complex chemical process called hydrogenation, in which liquid vegetable oils are heated to extremely high temperatures. This process causes some of the double bonds in the unsaturated oils to become single bonds. When this happens, the fat loses its curved shape and becomes a straight line. The straight-line shape of trans fats (like that of saturated fat) seems to be ideal for promoting the buildup of plaque in the arteries, which often leads to the onset of heart disease.

Until a few years ago, trans fats were widely found in many fried, packaged, and processed snack foods, baked goods, and entrées, such as chips, crackers, cookies, cakes, pastries, doughnuts, and frozen pizza. Recognition of their damaging effects on health has led to massive efforts by the food and restaurant industries to remove them from their products. Fortunately, trans fats are now gradually disappearing from many of the foods we eat. In fact, some major U.S. cities, including New York, Philadelphia, and Boston, have banned trans fats outright in restaurant meals.

However, many fast-food franchises continue to cook their food in unhealthy trans fat–laden frying fats and shortenings. In addition, most stick-type margarines still contain unhealthy amounts of trans fats. If you want to be sure that you are cutting down on the amount of trans fats you are consuming, check restaurants' nutrition guides for the trans fat content of their menu items, and replace hard stick-type margarines with soft tub spreads.

In addition, continue to check food labels to see if items contain partially hydrogenated oils, the source of trans fats in prepared and packaged foods. Be aware that some foods may contain these hydrogenated oils but still be labeled "0 trans fat." This is because the government allows food companies to label a product as trans fat–free or "not a significant source of trans fat" if it contains less than 0.50 gram of trans fat per serving. However, if you eat more than a few servings of the food, you may end up getting more trans fats than you think. The best bet is to avoid foods containing partially hydrogenated oils whenever possible.

So are you still wondering just how much fat you should be consuming? Although none of us can get away with unlimited amounts of fat in our diet, rest assured that fixating on the *amount* of fat in our food doesn't seem to be as important as we once thought. Focusing instead on cutting down on the bad trans and saturated fats, and increasing the good unsaturated fats, can be tremendously beneficial to our overall health.

Best Fat Choices: Olive and canola oils, soft "tub" margarines made with unsaturated vegetable oils, low-fat and skim dairy products. If you miss the taste of butter, try blending small amounts of it with olive oil.

Fruits and Vegetables

A walk down the produce aisle of the local supermarket reveals a feast for the eyes—stacks and stacks of gorgeously hued fruits and vegetables of nearly every size, shape, and description. Succulent tomatoes. Tangy bell peppers and crisp lettuce. Tart yellow-gold pears and maybe even a few unfamiliar things, like juicy star fruit or a deep crimson pomegranate. You get the idea. Fruits and vegetables are plentiful and diverse and offer us a truly unique sensory pleasure.

However, despite long-standing recommendations by numerous health agencies to eat more fruits and vegetables, most Americans fall woefully short in this area. Only about one-third of us get enough of either.

So why don't we eat more of them? There are probably many answers to this, but one of the main ones may be that we have lost some of our appreciation for the simple flavors and textures fruits and vegetables offer, due to our constant bombardment by heavily sugared, greased, and salted convenience foods. Another reason may be leftover messages from childhood—the notion that fruits and vegetables are good for us and therefore just *can't* taste good. Fortunately, it's never too late to learn to appreciate the wonderful and subtle flavors that fruits and vegetables provide.

Let's take a look at some of the many health benefits we get from fruits and vegetables. First off, eating them seems to protect against a wide variety of cancers (breast, stomach, colon, bladder, prostate, oral). Second, a diet rich in fruits and vegetables has been shown to fight heart disease, prevent stroke, and help lower blood pressure. Third, eating liberal amounts of them can help start us on the road to weight loss and then help us sustain it. Finally, eating more fruits and vegetables seems to improve everything from digestion to eyesight. In short, there doesn't seem to be any aspect of health that they don't improve.

How do fruits and vegetables accomplish so much? The answer lies in the great number and variety of nutrients they contain, which work both individually and together to keep us fit, healthy, and energetic. Here are some key components and their benefits:

- Water: Improves digestion, removes waste, and helps keep skin healthy and clear. Eating a serving or two of fruit or vegetables helps you get some of your daily water without even filling a glass.
- Vitamin C: A powerful antioxidant (see page 260).
- Beta-carotene (a type of vitamin A): May protect against many types of cancers.
- Potassium: Helps control blood pressure.
- Magnesium: Regulates heartbeat.
- Fiber: Lowers cholesterol, stabilizes blood sugar, and improves digestion.
- Folic acid: Helps prevent birth defects.
- Lycopene: A type of antioxidant that protects against prostate cancer.

- Polyphenols and bioflavonoids: Nutritional powerhouses that protect against many types of disease (see page 250).

So now that we know all the good things fruits and vegetables do for us, how much should we eat for maximum health?

The USDA *Dietary Guidelines for Americans, 2010* recommends eating nine or more servings of fruits and vegetables a day. Before you sink into your chair, daunted by this seemingly impossible goal, realize that a typical serving is quite small:

- One 2-inch apple, orange, or pear
- ½ cup applesauce or canned fruit
- ½–¾ cup berries or grapes
- ½ banana
- 1 cup melon
- ½ cup vegetable or fruit juice
- 1 cup lettuce or other raw greens
- ½ cup carrots, broccoli, green beans, or other cooked vegetable
- 1 small tomato

How do the nine servings of fruit and vegetables translate into a daily meal plan? Here is one example (as you can see, it is not difficult to fit nine servings into a day):

Breakfast: ½ sliced banana added to cereal, ½ glass orange juice (2 servings)

Lunch: Salad with 3 cups romaine lettuce and small sliced tomato (4 servings)

Snack: ¾ cup strawberries added to yogurt (1 serving)

Dinner: 1 cup steamed asparagus (2 servings)

Best Fruit and Vegetable Choices: All are excellent, but the deep green and orange types (spinach and other greens, carrots, sweet potatoes, mangoes, and papayas) have the highest amounts of vitamin A.

Fiber

Fiber gets a lot of airtime these days, mostly because of television advertising promoting a host of high-fiber supplements that promise "regularity." What exactly is fiber? Why do we need it, and where do we get it?

Also called "roughage," dietary fiber is the part of food that cannot be digested. It is found only in plant foods, such as fruits, vegetables, cereal grains, nuts, and seeds. Because it cannot be absorbed by the body, fiber has no calories and passes untouched through the intestinal tract, helping to speed up digestion.

Fiber can be described in a number of different ways, but it is most often defined as either soluble or insoluble. Soluble fiber has the ability to absorb water and form a gel in the intestine. As a result, it is able to slow down the rate of both glucose and cholesterol absorption, helping to create normal blood levels of both of these substances. Soluble fiber is found mostly in oats, barley, peas and beans, flaxseed, citrus fruit, and apples.

Insoluble fiber does not trap water in the intestine; instead, it passes unchanged through the intestinal tract, acting like a broom to push waste along. Insoluble fiber is found in wheat bran, whole wheat, fruits, vegetables, and nuts. This type of fiber helps prevent constipation and protects against a variety of gastrointestinal diseases like diverticulitis, irritable bowel syndrome, and colon cancer.

Also, because both types of fiber help provide a feeling of fullness, they may aid in weight loss.

How much fiber should we be consuming? Current national health guidelines encourage consuming 20 to 35 grams of fiber per day, about double the amount of most Americans' daily consumption.

The best way to increase fiber in your diet is to go slowly, adding small amounts of both types of fiber at a gradual pace (a few grams per day). Adding too much fiber too quickly can cause stomach upset, diarrhea, bloating, and gas.

The following table will give you an idea of the best sources of fiber:

HIGH-FIBER FOODS

FOOD	AMOUNT	FIBER (GRAMS)
Apple	1 medium	4.5
Asparagus	½ cup	1.8
Beans, black	½ cup	7.5
Beans, green	1 cup	3.8
Beans, kidney	½ cup	7.0
Blueberries	1 cup	3.6
Bran, oat	¼ cup	3.6
Bran, wheat	¼ cup	6.0
Bread, whole wheat	1 slice	2.0
Broccoli, cooked	½ cup	2.6
Carrot, raw	1 medium	1.7
Celery stalk	1 large	1.0
Cereal, All-Bran Bran Buds	⅓ cup	12.9
Cereal, Cheerios	1 cup	2.8
Cereal, raisin bran	1 cup	6.5
Cereal, shredded wheat	2 biscuits	4.6
Corn, cooked	1 cup	4.6
Crackers, whole wheat	6 crackers	3.0
Grapes	1 cup	1.4
Lentils, cooked	½ cup	7.8
Lettuce, iceberg	1 cup	0.7
Lettuce, romaine	1 cup	1.0
Oatmeal, regular, cooked	1 cup	4.0
Orange	1 medium	3.4
Peach	1 medium	2.2
Peanut butter, smooth	2 tablespoons	2.0
Peanuts	1 ounce	2.3

FOOD	AMOUNT	FIBER (GRAMS)
Pear	1 medium	5.5
Peas, cooked	½ cup	4.4
Potato, sweet, baked	1 medium	3.8
Potato, white, mashed	1 cup	2.5
Rice, brown	1 cup	3.5
Rice, white	1 cup	0.6
Spinach, cooked	1 cup	4.3
Tomato, raw	1 medium	1.5
Walnuts	½ cup	4.0

Source: USDA National Nutrient Database for Standard Reference, Release 23: http://www.nal.usda.gov/fnic/foodcomp/.

Water

Many of us don't think of water as a nutrient. Yet it may be one of the most important for health, and it is certainly necessary for survival. Did you know that there is no known life form on earth that can exist without water? In humans, water is essential for all of the body's processes, from digestion and absorption to brain function.

How much water do we need? According to the conventional wisdom, we need eight 8-ounce glasses a day for optimum health. Even to "hard-core" water drinkers, that amount can seem overwhelming. Where did that recommendation come from, and is it valid? Do we really need that much water?

The fact is, no one is really sure where the "8 glasses a day" rule came from. And, as a result, the question of whether we actually need to drink that much water remains hotly debated.

What is clear is that we need to drink at least enough water to replace bodily fluids lost through urine, breathing, and sweat. In healthy adults, this is about 6½ cups a day. Adding a little extra water to help with digestion and prevent dehydration will bring the daily water requirement close to the "8-glass" rule. People who are ill with diarrhea, vomiting, and/or fever, as well as heavy exercisers, need more.

Drinking too little water is a concern, especially for young children, who are more susceptible to the effects of dehydration, which are numerous and may include poor concentration and fatigue. In addition, drinking too little water can cause other physical ailments such as constipation, risk of kidney stones, and urinary tract infections. A few studies have even linked prolonged dehydration with a greater risk of cancer, though this has not been proved.

How do you know if you are dehydrated? One old rule of thumb for judging this is thirst—if you are thirsty, you are most likely dehydrated. However, thirst may be one of the body's last signals for communicating dehydration, so it's a good idea not to wait until you are thirsty before drinking something.

Another good rule is to check the color of your urine. If it is pale and colorless, chances are you are getting enough water; if not, you need to up your water intake.

Here are some conditions that may increase water needs:

- Airplane flights (the air inside the pressurized cabin of a plane is very dry).
- Working in an overheated or overly air-conditioned office.
- Working outside in extreme weather conditions—both hot, steamy weather and very cold weather can significantly increase our need for water. Thirst may be more noticeable on hot days, but be sure to remember to drink extra water on those frigid days as well.
- Exercise.

What about people who do lots of exercise? Although water needs vary among people, depending on age, weight, and state of health, a good rule of thumb is to drink 1 to 2 cups of water about 15 minutes before starting a workout. A cup of water should then be consumed every 20 minutes during vigorous exercise like running, hiking, and athletic competition. You may need even more if you are engaging in these activities on a hot day.

Many people cringe at the idea of trying to down so much water. Does all of our fluid have to come from water? The answer is no. We can also meet some of our water needs by drinking fruit juices, lemonade, and decaffeinated tea and coffee, and by eating fresh fruits and vegetables like apples, melons, and oranges and celery, cucumbers, and lettuce, which contain large amounts of water. Avoid alcohol and "regular" coffee and tea, because they tend to cause dehydration. In addition, it's important to remember that fruit juices contain large amounts of sugar and calories and may not be the best choice for those watching their weight.

It's important to note that heavy exercisers like marathon runners may need more than plain water to replace the salts their bodies lose through sweat. Replacing water without restoring the sodium and potassium that are lost in perspiration may be dangerous, since it can create a fluid overload in the body.

This raises the question: Is it possible to drink too much water? Yes, drinking large volumes of water can be dangerous, even deadly. However, the risk for most people drinking normal amounts of water is quite low. Those most at risk of "water poisoning" are heavy exercisers. This is why athletes engaged in endurance sports such as marathons must also replace lost body electrolytes in addition to water. This is easily done by drinking sports drinks like Gatorade that have balanced amounts of electrolytes added to them.

Sodium

For many years, sodium has been the "forgotten nutrient." Other than people on low-sodium diets, few of us have paid much attention to reducing our sodium intake, instead focusing on fat, sugar, and cholesterol.

But that is changing now. For the first time in years, the USDA *Dietary Guidelines for Americans, 2010* takes a look at sodium and has come up with a new recommendation. Not surprisingly, the new guideline reduces the target goal for daily sodium intake from 2,300 milligrams (about 1 teaspoon of salt) a day to 1,500 milligrams (¾ teaspoon). Since both amounts are far less than most of us consume (the typical

U.S. sodium intake is about 3,500 milligrams a day), it will be quite a challenge to meet this new goal.

Why was the guideline changed? The answer lies in the potentially negative effects of consuming too much sodium, including high blood pressure, kidney disease, heart failure, and stroke. By reducing the amount of dietary sodium to 1,500 milligrams a day (the amount we need to replace loss from sweat and to keep a normal fluid balance in our bodies), scientists hope that we can begin to lower the rates of these dangerous diseases.

It can be very difficult to know how much sodium we get from foods. Unlike the butter we spread on our toast and the sugar we add to our coffee, it's hard to see the sodium in our food, because most of it— about 75 percent—does not come from the salt we add while cooking or at the table; it comes from processed foods.

Below are the processed foods with the highest levels of sodium:

- Frozen pizza
- Snack foods
- White bread
- Processed cheese
- Hot dogs and cold cuts
- Jarred spaghetti sauce
- Ham
- Boxed rice mixes
- Canned soups
- Salad dressings
- Breakfast cereals

Fortunately, many food producers and manufacturers have begun to reduce the amounts of sodium they add to their products. Some of these reductions are as great as 50 percent, and, according to many food company representatives, do not compromise flavor. These new sodium-reduced products are now beginning to appear on grocery store shelves and should become more numerous within the next few years. Such products should make it easier for us to cut down on the total amount of sodium that we consume.

Experts agree that it is easiest to slowly reduce the amount of sodium we consume than to try to immediately eliminate all excess salt from our diet. Here are some practical suggestions for gradually reducing your sodium intake:

- Look for snack and convenience foods that are labeled "reduced sodium" or "low sodium."
- Limit how many processed foods you eat; stick to your favorites and eliminate those that are "just a habit."
- Avoid packaged and processed foods with very high amounts of sodium. These will have 20 percent or more of the daily value for sodium.
- Try to ease up on the salt shaker. Even though salt added in cooking or at the table amounts to only 15 percent of our total sodium intake, resisting the urge to salt everything on your plate can help you cut down.

Some Really Super Nutrients

Antioxidants, polyphenols, bioflavonoids, phytochemicals, lignans—these and other mysterious-sounding nutrients seem to be everywhere lately—talked about on the news, touted on food labels, and bandied about in discussions of health. Many people wonder, "Just what in the world are these things, and what do they do?"

Although they vary in their chemical makeup and in the way they work, all of the nutrients listed above have very powerful effects on health. All are potent fighters against cancer and heart disease. In addition, many of them help build immunity, regulate blood sugar levels, combat inflammation, improve blood pressure and circulation, and kill bacteria and fungi.

An *antioxidant* is a molecule that is able to stop dangerous unstable compounds called free radicals from damaging cells. Free radicals are present in cigarette smoke and environmental pollution and are also formed as a natural part of our own metabolism. They can cause damage to our bodies by attacking and changing the DNA in our cells. Antioxidants stop damage from free radicals by preventing a destructive chemical reaction known as oxidation—hence their name.

Polyphenols are compounds with complex structures that are widely found in plant foods. Many are pigments that are responsible for the brilliant colors of fruits and vegetables and have antioxidant properties.

Bioflavonoids are a type of polyphenol that are found in tea, coffee, and cocoa, as well as in fruits and vegetables.

Phytochemicals are also complex plant-based compounds that are found in herbs and medicinal plants as well as in fruits and vegetables.

Lignans are a type of phytochemical found in flaxseed and other seeds, soybeans, and cereal grains.

Many of these nutrients are powerful cancer fighters.

Ten Superfoods

Superfoods are those that contain large amounts of vitamins, minerals, antioxidants, bioflavonoids, and other nutrients that protect against disease and keep us healthy. It's important to remember that there are many such foods to choose from, and that eating a variety of them is encouraged. Below are ten of these nutritional powerhouses and some of the health benefits they provide:

Blueberries: How can something that tastes so good be good for you? Blueberries contain some of the highest levels of bioflavonoids, which are known to boost immunity and protect against disease, including cancer, heart disease, and high blood pressure. In addition, studies are beginning to show that eating blueberries fights some of the declines in memory and learning ability that come with aging.

Onion: The lowly onion is the exception that proves the rule. Although it is not brightly colored, it is packed with the two powerful bioflavonoids *quercetin* and *isorhamnetin,* which may help lower blood pressure, and have been shown to kill cancer cells in animals.

Olive oil: Olive oil contains large amounts of the two antioxidants *tyrosol* and *hydroxytyrosol,* as well as an organic compound called oleocanthal, which reduces inflammation. Olive oil is also one of the richest sources of monounsaturated fat, which is good for our hearts, and may also combat arthritis and asthma.

Walnuts: Like blueberries, walnuts have been shown to fight off some of the mental decline of aging. They are a very good source of omega-3 fats, which are beneficial for heart health.

Tomatoes: About ten years ago, a number of studies showed that tomatoes could help prevent or slow prostate cancer. Recent research has also shown that tomatoes may decrease the risk of many other types of cancers as well. A powerful antioxidant called lycopene, which gives tomatoes their brilliant red color, is believed to be responsible for this.

Spices and herbs: It is difficult to name just one spice, since virtually all of them seem to offer some sort of health benefit. Most of them appear to be able to kill bacteria and molds and to help control blood clotting. Curry powder and turmeric are spices that are widely used in Indian cooking. They contain *curcumin,* which has been shown to fight off the *H. pylori* bacteria that cause stomach cancer and ulcers. Cinnamon contains compounds that kill the microbes in foods that may lead to certain types of food poisoning. Oregano, much beloved in Italian cuisine, contains high levels of *rosmarinic acid,* an antioxidant that boosts immunity and shows promise for helping the symptoms of rheumatoid arthritis.

Oats: If you have seen the TV commercials touting the wonders of oatmeal, you probably know that oats can help lower cholesterol. In addition, the fiber in oats can help keep blood sugar levels healthy and stable. Oats also contain a special kind of antioxidant named ferulic acid. Found mostly in grains, ferulic acid may help strengthen bones and protect against many types of cancer; it even seems to protect cells against damage from UV light.

Sesame seeds: Sesame seeds contain large amounts of lignans, which have something called phytoestrogenic activity; that is, they help balance the activity of estrogen in the body and may help fight breast, ovarian, and uterine cancers.

Dark chocolate: You really can't say enough good things about dark chocolate. It contains enormous amounts of a variety of bioflavonoids and other healthful compounds that not only protect against disease, but also help improve mood and fight memory loss. (For the record, milk chocolate also contains some of these substances, but only about 25 percent of the amounts found in dark chocolate.) But even though dark chocolate is really good for us, it is still high in calories, so we can't consume unlimited amounts of it. For most people, eating an ounce a day is fine.

Tea: Tea is loaded with *theaflavins,* a type of bioflavonoid that increases immunity and may help to fight off dementia. Although green tea contains the highest amounts, black tea is also a great source of these bioflavonoids.

Brain Food

Yes, there really are foods that can make us smarter—or at least improve our memories and fight off the negative effects on mental capacity that come with aging. Eating for brain health is a new and exciting area of nutrition that offers great promise for keeping us mentally sharp and lucid well into our senior years.

In order to understand how food can boost brain power, it's useful to look at some of the changes that happen in our brains as we get older. To start with, as we age, our brains become smaller (we lose 15 to 20 percent of brain weight between the ages of twenty and ninety), while the number of damaged or destroyed neurons (brain cells) increases. In addition, levels of key brain chemicals that handle the processes of learning and memory begin to decrease. These changes come about in part as a result of inflammation brought on by poor diet, smoking, lack of exercise, and stress. In addition, free radicals (those dangerous compounds that attack and damage cells) can wreak havoc on brain cells. All of these forces contribute to the decline in memory and in mental ability that often comes with aging.

So how and where does food fit into this picture? Scientists now know that there are a variety of foods that contain nutrients that are able to fight off these negative changes in the brain. Some of these nutrients are antioxidants, which work to kill off free radicals, while others seem to have the ability to increase blood flow, spur on the growth of new brain cells, and help neurons communicate with one another.

Not surprisingly, these brain-boosting foods are also listed in the "superfoods" section above: blueberries, walnuts, dark chocolate, and tea.

The degree to which these foods can actually slow down the ravaging effects of aging on our brains is still not clear. However, studies in both lab animals and people have shown that eating more of them improves memory, physical coordination, and simple reasoning.

How much of these foods do we have to eat to improve our brain function? More research is needed in this area, but eating as little as an ounce of walnuts or a cup of blueberries a day may help do the trick. Good news, indeed, for all of us who want to keep our mental abilities sharp.

Glycemic Index

Over the past ten years, a lot of media attention has been paid to something called the glycemic index. Simply put, the glycemic index (GI) is a ranking of the effects of different carbohydrates on our blood sugar levels. These rankings range from 0 to 100, with white bread having a GI of 75 and glucose a GI of 100.

Because they are slowly absorbed by the body, low-GI foods tend to help keep blood sugar levels low. High-GI foods, on the other hand, are rapidly digested and absorbed and can therefore cause unhealthy spikes in blood sugar. Keeping blood sugar levels stable and within normal range is important for everyone, not just diabetics. This is because prolonged levels of very high blood sugar can eventually lead to or worsen serious health conditions such as heart disease.

In addition, eating foods with low GI values can help us lose weight and improve blood cholesterol levels.

How is GI measured? The GI value of a food is calculated by feeding small groups of healthy people a portion of the food containing 50 grams of carbohydrates and then measuring the effect on their blood glucose levels over the next 2 hours. These results are then compared with the blood responses of the people in the study to a dose of glucose that has the same amount of carbohydrates as the food being tested.

Low-GI foods tend to be fruits and vegetables, unprocessed carbohydrates and cereals, nuts, beans, and most dairy products, while high-GI foods tend to be high in sugar and/or starch. Protein foods like meat, fish, and eggs contain no carbohydrates, and therefore have a GI of zero.

The following table shows some examples of foods with a low, medium, and high GI:

LOW-GI FOODS	
FOOD	GI
Hummus	6
Peanuts	7
Tomato, raw	8
Barley	22
Peach	28
Apple	30
Bran cereal	30
Chocolate	35
Orange	40
Milk	40
Oatmeal	45
MEDIUM-GI FOODS	
FOOD	GI
Yogurt	50
Ice cream	60
Banana	60
Corn, boiled	60
Cherries	63
Brown rice	66
Raisins	65
Wheat crackers	65
Pizza	65
Pineapple	66

HIGH-GI FOODS	
FOOD	GI
Corn chips	75
Doughnut	76
Watermelon	80
White rice	80
Pancake	80
Jelly beans	80
Rice cake	82
Cornflakes	83
Pretzel	84
Mashed potato	85
Source: GI Database: http://www.glycemicindex.com.	

To date, hundreds of foods have been tested for their GI response. Some of the rankings of the foods may seem surprising. For example, chocolate has a low GI (35), while watermelon has a fairly high GI (80). This is because the GI of a food is affected by many different factors.

Chocolate has a high fat content, which acts to lower its effect on blood sugar. Watermelon, on the other hand, contains simple sugars, which are rapidly absorbed and can push blood sugar levels up. Other factors that may affect a food's GI are how it is processed and cooked, and the amounts of fiber and starch it contains.

Trying to eat more low-GI foods and fewer high-GI foods makes good sense for all of us. By avoiding repeated spikes in blood sugar, we can help our bodies work more efficiently and perhaps reduce the risk of becoming overweight or developing diabetes down the road.

Low-Calorie Sweeteners

Once limited to diet sodas, low-calorie sweeteners (sometimes called "artificial sweeteners" or "sugar substitutes") are now making their way into a wide variety of foods and beverages, from breakfast cereals to fruit juices. In addition, there are a number of different types of low-calorie sweeteners used in foods today. Because of this, we now consume more of these sweeteners than we ever did in the past.

There are many different reasons for the increase in popularity of these sweeteners. The most obvious one is that many people are watching their calories and see low-calorie sweeteners as a convenient and easy way to decrease the calories they get from sugar. In addition, diabetics who are restricting their sugar intake find that low-calorie sweeteners can offer an alternative way to satisfy a sweet tooth.

Low-calorie sweeteners are synthetic substances that do not contain calories, and that are not absorbed by the body (with a few exceptions). In general, they are many times sweeter than sugar; for this reason, they can be used in very small amounts in food products to give the same degree of sweetness that sugar provides, without the calories.

All low-calorie sweeteners must be approved by the FDA before they can be introduced to the food supply. Approval of a low-calorie sweetener follows years of studies that look at risk of disease, particularly cancer. In addition, the FDA sets safe consumption levels for all of the sweeteners it approves.

Deciphering the names of low-calorie sweeteners on food labels can be quite challenging. To help clear up the confusion, let's look at the ones now used in the United States:

Aspartame is probably the best known of the low-calorie sweeteners. It has been in use in the United States since 1981, mostly in diet sodas, fruit juice drinks, breakfast cereals, yogurt, and frozen desserts. It is also in the packaged sweetener Equal, found in the familiar blue packets on restaurant tables, and in NutraSweet. One disadvantage of aspartame is that it cannot be used in cooking, since high heat destroys its sweetening ability.

Aspartame is made of the two amino acids phenylalanine and aspartic acid, which are broken down into harmless substances by most people's digestive systems. However, individuals who suffer from the rare genetic disease phenylketonuria (PKU) cannot metabolize phenylalanine and therefore need to avoid consuming all foods and beverages sweetened with aspartame. Products containing this sweetener must be clearly labeled to inform consumers about its risk to people with phenylketonuria.

Acesulfame potassium, or Ace-K, is a popular sweetener that has been used in the United States since 1988. It is used in diet sodas and other beverages, baked goods and other foods, and chewing gum. It is also found in the packaged sweeteners Sweet One and Sunétt.

Unlike aspartame, Ace-K is not broken down and is passed through the body intact. Because it can stand up to high heat, Ace-K can be used in cooking.

Saccharin is one of the oldest low-calorie sweeteners and is widely used in the United States. It is also one of the most controversial of the low-calorie sweeteners and has been closely studied to see if consuming it is linked with increased cancer risk. Because very large amounts of saccharin (equal to about 10,000 tablets a day) have been found to cause bladder cancer in lab animals, food products containing it must carry warning labels. However, studies in humans have not found any link between saccharin use and cancer. Saccharin is used in diet soda, fruit drinks, chewing gum, dessert items, and jams and jellies. It is probably best known as the sweetener found in one of the first diet sodas, Tab, and is also found in the popular packaged sugar substitute Sweet'n Low.

Sucralose was approved for use in the United States in 1998. Like the other low-calorie sweeteners, it is used in diet soda and other beverages, yogurt, and prepared baked goods, but it can also be used in baking and cooking. It is one of the most intense of the low-calorie sweeteners, with a sweetening power 600 times greater than sugar.

Sorbitol is not usually included with other low-calorie sweeteners, since it contains some calories and is absorbed in small amounts by the body. However, it is now widely used in many food products, especially chewing gum and sugar-free diabetic products, and deserves discussion. Sorbitol is a sugar alcohol that is found naturally in fruits such as prunes, apples, and pears, and that is also made commercially. Because it is only about half as sweet as table sugar, it is usually used with other low-calorie sweeteners. Because consuming too much sorbitol may cause digestive upset, foods containing it must carry a warning label to that effect. Other types of sugar alcohols that are also used as sweeteners in foods include *mannitol, xylitol,* and *maltitol.*

As mentioned earlier, the FDA sets safe levels of consumption for low-calorie sweeteners. These levels are called acceptable daily intakes (ADIs) and are based on body weight. The ADIs set by the FDA range from 5 to 50 milligrams per kilogram of body weight, which translates into 20 to 30 cans of diet soda per day, obviously much more than a person would ever drink. So go ahead and enjoy your diet soda—just remember to drink other fluids as well.

Vitamins, Supplements, and Herbs

Americans spend billions of dollars each year on vitamins and supplements—over $5 billion in 2009 on herbs alone—and the trend shows no sign of slowing down. The most popular supplements include multivitamins with minerals; vitamins A, C, D, and E; calcium; zinc; B-complex vitamins; fish oils; coenzyme Q10; and glucosamine/chondroitin. Among herbs, ginkgo biloba, Saint-John's-wort, ginseng, echinacea, and evening primrose oil are the top sellers.

Are vitamins and other dietary supplements necessary? Do they provide extra health benefits that we can't get from food?

It is difficult to answer these questions without having a basic understanding of what vitamins, supplements, and herbal preparations do and don't do, and how they relate to the food we eat. Several important guidelines apply when we are considering using any vitamin, supplement, or herb:

- Vitamin and dietary supplements and herbs sold in the United States are not closely regulated by the FDA. Therefore, judging their safety and effectiveness can be difficult. Buy only from established manufacturers with a reputable history.
- There may be dangerous interactions and side effects when you take different combinations of supplements and/or herbs. This is especially true when these are taken with prescription medications. Some of these negative effects are well known, but some have not been explored. Because of this, it's important to read the product information carefully, to take the lowest possible doses, and to discuss using them with your doctor, especially if you use prescription drugs.

- Because there is no comprehensive government regulation of dietary supplements, it's nearly impossible to know about the purity and strength of many of the supplements you buy. This is particularly true for herbal supplements. Your best defense here is to check labels and look for the term *standardized* or *guaranteed potency* on the label. Although not a foolproof guarantee, this means that the product has met some basic standards for quality control.
- Supplements cannot take the place of a good diet! It's important to get as many of our nutrients as possible from foods, since whole, intact foods offer many benefits that are missing from individual supplements. This may be especially true for powdered fruit and vegetable extracts and supplements. It is impossible to know how the manufacturing process affects the purity and nutritional quality of these types of products.

Despite the general lack of knowledge about the safety and effectiveness of many supplements, the National Institutes of Health (NIH) has established recommended dietary allowances (RDAs), also known as dietary reference intakes (DRIs), for many vitamins and minerals. (*Dietary reference intakes* is a newer term that is not yet appearing on supplement labels, so to keep things simple, we'll refer here to the allowances as RDAs.)

The RDAs for vitamins and minerals vary by age and sex and represent the average intake levels that are believed to meet the nutritional needs of most healthy people. In many cases, the amounts of vitamins and minerals found in commercial supplements are much greater than the RDAs, so it's important to know the safe levels of intakes before taking these products. There are no RDAs for herbs, though we do have some knowledge about safe intake levels for them.

Let's look at some of the popular vitamin supplements and see how they stack up against the RDAs and what they might offer in terms of health benefits.

Multivitamin and mineral supplements: These are by far one of the most popular types of supplements sold in the United States. They generally contain a variety of vitamins and minerals known to be essential for health, usually in doses two to three times the RDAs.

Vitamin A: Vitamin A is a fat-soluble vitamin (meaning it can be stored in the body). It has several important functions, including keeping vision and skin healthy. Vitamin A is found both in animal foods (eggs, liver, and dairy products) and in fruits and vegetables, such as carrots, spinach, and papayas, in which it is called beta-carotene. The RDA for vitamin A for adult men is 5,000 international units (IUs); for adult women, it is 4,000 IUs. Commercial vitamin A supplements may contain as much as five times these amounts. Because vitamin A is easily stored and can build up to unhealthy levels in the body, it's a good idea to avoid taking vitamin A supplements that provide more than the RDA.

Vitamin C: Probably everyone has heard that vitamin C prevents and lessens the symptoms of colds. While this has never been proved to be true, vitamin C does help the body fight infection. It is also a powerful antioxidant that helps combat the free radicals that damage cells. Vitamin C is classified as a water-soluble vitamin (meaning it is not stored in the body). It is found in citrus fruits, peppers, and tomatoes, and its RDA is set at 90 milligrams per day for men and 75 milligrams for women. Many vitamin C supplements contain much higher amounts: 1,000 milligrams or more. There is really no known benefit to taking these amounts; in fact, taking too much vitamin C over a period of time can cause kidney stones and problems with the immune system. Making sure to eat a few servings of foods rich in vitamin C each day is the best way to ensure we are getting enough.

Vitamin D: Vitamin D is a fat-soluble vitamin that helps keep bones strong and healthy. It is found in a very limited number of foods: fortified milk and breakfast cereals, and fatty fish such as salmon. Our bodies can also make vitamin D from moderate exposure to sunlight; however, people living in northern climates with limited sun exposure during the winter months will produce very low amounts. As a result of inadequate sunlight and few food sources, many adults fail to get the RDA of 400 IUs. Therefore, it makes sense for most of us to take a multivitamin containing vitamin D or to take a vitamin D supplement that meets the RDA.

Vitamin E: Vitamin E is a fat-soluble vitamin and antioxidant that may protect against cancer and heart disease. Some studies have also shown that vitamin E may protect against Alzheimer's disease. The RDA for adults is 15 milligrams per day. Like vitamin D, vitamin E is found in a limited number of foods (wheat germ, sunflower seeds, nuts, and vegetable oils), and therefore it is hard to get enough from diet alone. Taking a multivitamin supplement that contains vitamin E or a vitamin E supplement that provides the RDA is the best way to make sure we get enough.

Calcium: Calcium works with vitamin D to build bone and keep it strong. In addition, it helps to regulate heartbeat and many other bodily functions. The RDA for calcium for adults is 1,000 milligrams a day, and people over the age of fifty need more (1,200 milligrams) to guard against bone loss. Dairy foods are the best source of calcium, but some people find it difficult to eat the 3 to 4 servings a day necessary to meet the RDA. Taking a calcium supplement can be a good way to make sure that we are getting the calcium we need. It's important that dietary and supplemental calcium also be balanced with enough vitamin D, which helps the body absorb calcium.

Zinc: Zinc is a mineral that helps promote normal growth and development, fights infection, and aids in wound healing. It also helps us maintain appetite and a normal sense of taste and smell. The RDA for zinc is 11 milligrams a day for men and 8 milligrams for women. Zinc is available from a variety of foods (meats, seafood, wheat germ, and fortified breakfast cereals), but vegetarians and "picky eaters" may not get enough from their diets. Taking a multivitamin supplement with added zinc is the best way to ensure that we are getting enough. Zinc supplements may vary a lot in their dosages, so if you decide to take one, it is a good idea to choose a brand that is close to the RDA.

B-complex vitamins: B-complex vitamins are popular and usually include seven types of B vitamins: thiamin (B_1), riboflavin (B_2), niacin (B_3), pantothenic acid (B_3) pyridoxine (B_6), vitamin B_{12}, and folic acid. Some B-complex preparations also include biotin and choline. The B vitamins are responsible for helping to convert food into energy and also protect against some kinds of anemia. In addition, folic acid may offer protection against heart disease. The B-complex vitamins are all water soluble, and they are generally needed in small amounts. Thanks to food fortification, B-complex vitamins are found in many foods, particularly breakfast cereals and enriched grain products, so most people can get more than enough from the foods they eat.

Fish oils, coenzyme Q10, glucosamine/chondroitin, and herbs like ginkgo biloba and Saint-John's-wort are not vitamins or minerals and do not have RDAs. However, they are among the most popular supplements sold in the United States, and some may offer unique nutritional benefits.

Fish oils: Fish oils contain large amounts of beneficial omega-3 fatty acids, which have been shown to protect against heart disease. Omega-3 fatty acids have also been shown to prevent heart arrhythmias, in which the heart beats out of control. The general recommendation for increasing omega-3 fatty acids in our diets is to eat fatty fish like salmon, herring, and sardines several times a week. However, for those who are not fond of seafood, fish oil supplements can be a good alternative, though we still don't know if the oils offer all of the benefits that we get from eating the whole fish. Unless larger amounts are prescribed by your doctor, limiting fish oil supplements to doses of 1 gram seems to make sense.

Coenzyme Q10: Coenzyme Q10 (also known as "coenzyme Q") is a widely used supplement that is believed to protect against cancer and heart disease, prevent migraine headaches, and improve periodontal health. However, none of these claims has been proved, and the benefits of coenzyme Q10 supplementation are unknown. In addition, it is unlikely that healthy people will develop deficiencies in conezyme Q10, since it is found in many foods (including meat, fish, poultry, avocados, and parsley) and is also manufactured by our bodies.

Glucosamine/chondroitin: Glucosamine and chondroitin sulfate are natural substances that make up cartilage, a type of connective tissue that is found between bones. Taken together as a supplement, they have been shown in some studies to reduce the swelling and pain of osteoarthritis, a chronic joint disease caused by breakdown of cartilage. Because glucosamine and chondroitin supplements have few and/or mild side effects, there is little harm in taking them for pain relief from arthritis.

Ginkgo biloba is one of the top-selling herbs in the United States. It is most often used to enhance concentration and improve memory, as well as to fight the effects of Alzheimer's disease. However, solid evidence for its effectiveness is spotty. In addition, ginkgo biloba may have side effects, such as headaches, dizziness, nausea, vomiting, and irregular heartbeat. It may also interact negatively with prescription medications. So if you take ginkgo biloba, it makes sense to use the lowest dose possible.

Saint-John's-wort is an herb that is used to treat mild to moderate depression and is widely prescribed in some countries, such as Germany, to treat this disorder. Some studies have found that doses of about 1,000 milligrams of Saint-John's-wort show promise in easing the symptoms of depression. Although Saint-John's-wort has few side effects, it is important to discuss using it with your doctor before you begin taking it.

Ginseng is a Chinese herb that is used to treat fatigue and weakness, and to increase energy. In addition, it may show promise in helping regulate blood sugar levels. However, taking more than a few hundred milligrams a day may lead to restlessness and insomnia.

Echinacea is used to treat colds, flu, and other types of respiratory illnesses. Results of studies looking at the effectiveness of this herb have been mixed, with some showing no effect and others showing some real benefit as a treatment for upper respiratory tract infections. Echinacea does not seem to have serious side effects, though some people may experience skin rashes and stomach upset. In addition, people with asthma may be more prone to asthmatic attacks when taking echinacea.

Evening primrose is a popular supplement that is used to treat eczema and inflammatory disorders such as arthritis. It is also widely used by women to prevent or lessen symptoms of menopause and premenstrual syndrome (PMS). Because of its high levels of a beneficial fatty acid called gamma-linolenic acid (GLA), evening primrose oil may also protect against breast cancer. Evening primrose oil has few serious side effects, but may interfere with prescription medications that affect blood clotting.

These are just a few of the vitamin and herbal supplements available today. Many have the ability to positively affect health and well-being, while others should be used cautiously, with a doctor's approval. Before taking any new supplement, be sure to learn as much about it as you can, and to start with the lowest effective dose. And remember, foods are always the preferred way to get the nutrients we need.

Probiotics

Have you heard of probiotics? Have you wondered what they are, what the buzz is about, and what sort of health benefits they might hold for you?

If so, you are not alone. Probiotics, sold in both food and supplemental form, represent one of the fastest-growing segments of the nutritional products market.

Although there are differences of opinions as to how to define *probiotics,* one commonly accepted definition, provided by the World Health Organization (WHO), is that they are "live microorganisms, which, when administered in adequate amounts, confer a health benefit on the host." Translated into plain English, this means that they are tiny bugs (usually bacteria) that are good for our health. Unlike "bad" bacteria that cause illnesses and diseases, the good probiotic bugs may actually protect us from getting sick. Although probiotics are a new concept to most Americans, they have been in use for thousands of years.

Before talking about probiotics in foods and supplements, it's important to remember that the human body produces its own mix of good bacteria that help to fight off unfriendly disease-causing invaders, such as bad bacteria, molds, yeasts, and parasites. These good bacteria live in our mouths, on our skin, and in our digestive tracts. Most of the time, they do a phenomenal job of keeping us healthy, but sometimes they can become unbalanced—usually as a result of illness, infection, and/or prolonged antibiotic use, which tends to wipe out the good bugs that live inside us.

Most probiotic bacteria found in foods and supplements come from the genus *Lactobacillus* and the genus *Bifidobacterium,* and each of these categories has its own particular species and varieties. One type of probiotic bacteria that is fairly well known to many people is *Lactobacillus acidophilus,* found in yogurt. Probiotic bacteria are also found in kefir and other types of fermented milk products, as well as in soy foods like miso and tempeh.

In addition to foods, probiotics are also sold in supplement form. Probiotic supplements may contain one or more strains of probiotic bacteria and are usually sold as capsules, with a typical dose being 1 or 2 capsules per day. According to product labels, one dose of a probiotic supplement may provide a billion or more CFUs—colony-forming units. This term refers to its ability to achieve a normal balance of bacteria in the digestive tract.

So why do people use probiotics? Below are some of the health benefits people seek from probiotics:

- To treat diarrhea caused by lactose intolerance, antibiotic use, or other factors
- To relieve the symptoms of inflammatory bowel disease (IBD) and irritable bowel syndrome (IBS)
- To treat stomach infections brought on by *H. pylori,* a type of bacteria known to cause stomach ulcers and gastritis
- To improve digestive upset caused by food intolerance or allergy

Do probiotics work? For many people, probiotics seem to provide great relief from their gastrointestinal distress. In addition, studies are now under way to evaluate the effectiveness of probiotics in combating other types of diseases, such as bladder cancer and the often deadly hospital-acquired bacterial infection *Clostridium difficile.*

Although probiotic supplements are safe and show promise in helping people with gastrointestinal problems, they are not without side effects. In sensitive individuals, they may cause stomach upset, gas, and bloating. As with all nutritional supplements, it's important to follow the dosage instructions, and to discontinue use if you experience lasting or severe side effects. In addition, probiotic use may not be suitable for people with lowered immunity due to chronic illness or infection, or for the elderly and children.

Finally, probiotic supplements can be costly. Those wishing to benefit from the action of probiotics may find that eating yogurt and other food sources regularly provides satisfactory results.

Energy Bars and Drinks

Just like vitamin and herbal supplements, energy bars and drinks have exploded into the U.S. food market. At last count, there were dozens of these products on the market, and their numbers continue to grow.

The term *energy bar* is a catchall, since these products vary a lot in their nutritional quality, ingredients, and purpose. There are low-carb, high-carb, high-protein, and low-fat varieties, as well as bars that are highly supplemented with vitamins and minerals.

Energy drinks tend to contain large amounts of sugar and caffeine and may also contain B vitamins, taurine (an amino acid that reportedly enhances athletic performance), and herbs like ginseng and guarana.

Do these products work? Certainly they provide quick calories and a pick-me-up in the middle of the day or before a workout. However, there really isn't a lot of evidence that energy bars and drinks are superior to "regular" foods when it comes to providing fuel for exercise. While energy bars are safe, they are expensive and are often loaded with large amounts of calories and sugar. They may be suitable for athletes who burn off calories while taking part in high-intensity or endurance sports, but for most people, they are generally unnecessary and best limited to occasional snacks. If you do have a fondness for energy bars, it makes sense to choose ones that have the lowest amounts of sugar, and that also have some added vitamins and minerals.

And what about energy drinks? Many people who use them report feeling more alert and having increased endurance during workouts. It may be that this is mostly due to caffeine, which has well-known stimulant effects. Most energy drinks contain amounts of caffeine similar to those found in brewed coffee (100 to 160 milligrams per 8 ounces). However, the caffeine in these products may combine with the other added stimulants to provide a powerful "kick" in excess of what one gets from a cup of coffee. There have been reports of people experiencing "caffeine overload" when consuming these drinks. Reactions to excess caffeine include sleeplessness, jittery nerves, and irregular heartbeat, which may be dangerous in sensitive individuals. Therefore, it makes sense to limit the amount of energy drinks that you consume (especially if you are a coffee drinker). Above all, energy drinks should never be consumed by children, or pregnant or nursing women. In addition, individuals taking prescription drugs such as blood pressure medication should check with their doctor before using these products.

So what can you eat before a workout to provide your body with energy?

Here are some suggestions for beverages and snacks that are both healthy and delicious:

- ½ cup cereal with a banana
- Yogurt with strawberries
- Low-fat granola bar
- Whole wheat crackers with peanut butter
- A homemade smoothie made with milk or soy milk, juice, and fruit
- Fruit juice
- Lemonade
- Water
- Gatorade (especially important for people sweating a great deal while exercising)

Vegetarianism

Vegetarian diets, once considered a weird lifestyle practiced by bearded, barefoot hippies, are now one of the hottest dietary trends in the United States. Mainstream grocery stores now devote entire sections to food products catering to vegetarians, meatless entrées are found everywhere from airplanes to restaurants, and vegetarian cookbooks are popular sellers.

A 2008 study showed that about 3 percent of the U.S. population (7 million people) were vegetarians, and another 10 percent (23 million) followed a diet influenced by vegetarian habits. About 1 million Americans considered themselves to be "vegan," meaning that they consumed no animal products at all. These are astonishing numbers, in light of the fact that as recently as 20 years ago vegetarianism was considered an oddity.

Why this increased interest in vegetarianism?

There is no doubt that many reasons are driving this trend, but some of the main ones are a growing awareness of environmental concerns and "green" eating, a desire to improve health, an interest in animal welfare, and the skyrocketing costs of meat and other animal foods.

Exactly what is a vegetarian diet? Simply put, vegetarians avoid eating meat, poultry, and fish. In addition to vegans, who avoid all animal foods, there are lacto-vegetarians (those who consume dairy products) and lacto-ovo vegetarians (those who eat both dairy products and eggs).

With a few exceptions, such as soy, only animal foods supply complete proteins—those containing all of the amino acids we need for growth and repair of body tissues. Proteins from plant foods are limited in the number and variety of amino acids they contain. For this reason, vegetarians must combine different types of plant foods with complementary amino acids in order to "create" complete proteins.

Here are some examples of complementary protein combinations:

- Whole wheat bread with peanut butter
- Black beans and rice
- Pasta tossed with sesame seeds
- Split pea soup with crackers
- Tofu with brown rice

It was once believed that complementary protein foods needed to be eaten at the same time in order to provide complete protein. Now we know that eating foods with complementary foods on the same day is sufficient to provide the benefit of complete protein.

Given the variety in the types of vegetarian diets, it's not surprising that they can vary tremendously in their nutritional value. As with all types of diets, the most restricted vegetarian diets present a risk of being deficient in some nutrients. The nutrients that are most likely to be low on a vegetarian diet are calcium, vitamin D, iron, zinc, and vitamin B_{12}. However, with some knowledge and planning, virtually any vegetarian diet can be a healthy one.

Though we think of dairy foods as being the primary source of calcium and vitamin D, orange juice, rice milk, and soy milk that are fortified with these nutrients can meet the needs of the vegetarian. Vegetarians can also get calcium from cooked collard greens and tofu prepared with calcium, while zinc is found in tahini, pumpkin seeds, beans, and lentils. Because only animal foods contain vitamin B_{12}, vegetarians need to get their B_{12} from supplements or foods fortified with B_{12}, like soy milk. In addition, fortified breakfast cereals are an excellent source of all these nutrients. Perhaps the best assurance of getting enough of these nutrients is to take a daily multivitamin supplement.

Growing children and teenagers have unique nutritional needs such as extra calories and protein, and many vitamins and minerals. These needs can be challenging to meet on a vegetarian diet. However, as with adults, a bit of knowledge and careful planning can ensure that kids get the nutrients they need from meatless diets. Making sure they eat a variety of complementary protein foods and take the needed vitamin and mineral supplements will help ensure that they get what they need for normal growth and development.

There is little doubt that eating a vegetarian diet can provide many health benefits. However, it is not necessary to completely eliminate meat and other animal foods in order to reap some of the benefits of a vegetarian lifestyle. By simply eating less of these foods, we can help control our weight, lower our blood cholesterol levels, improve digestion, and significantly lower our risk of heart disease and many types of cancers. Remember that little changes make a big difference!

Food Additives

It's no exaggeration to say that our food is loaded with additives. Reading the ingredient list of nearly any packaged food in the grocery store can be like a bewildering excursion into a chemistry lab: Bulking agents, emulsifiers, colors and dyes, sweeteners, preservatives, thickeners, stabilizers, and texturizers are just some of the stuff you may find on a food label. Slogging through a long list of food additives may make you wonder how the manufacturer found any room for a food at all!

Many of us are concerned (with good reason) about the amounts and types of additives that are routinely put into our foods. Although many food additives are safe, some are questionable. There are several things to remember when you are trying to make sense of the additives listed on a food label.

The more processed a food is, the more likely it is to contain a long list of additives. Therefore, eating fresh food close to its natural state is the best way to avoid consuming these additives.

All food additives have to be approved by the Food and Drug Administration (FDA) before they can be used. The stamp of approval bestowed by the FDA is known as GRAS ("generally regarded as safe"). Right now over 2,000 food additives are approved for use by the FDA.

Not all food additives are synthetic chemicals. In fact, some are natural and contribute to the food's nutritional quality. An example of this would be vitamin C that is sometimes added to jarred and prepackaged fruits to keep them fresh.

The vast majority of additives are used in very small amounts in foods—usually less than 0.5 percent of the total weight of a food. As a result, our overall consumption of them tends to be quite low.

There are a handful of commonly used food additives that may have questionable effects on health. Because of this, it would make sense to avoid consuming too many foods that contain them. This holds true especially for children and pregnant and nursing women.

What are the food additives that we need to be aware of? The following is a list of some (all on the FDA's GRAS list) that have raised safety concerns.

Sodium benzoate: Sodium benzoate is a preservative that is used in salad dressings, carbonated sodas, pickles, jams, and fruit juices, and also in mouthwashes and liquid medications. Some scientists believe that it can damage the DNA in body cells, and other researchers think it may contribute to hyperactivity in children.

Benzoic acid: Like its cousin sodium benzoate, benzoic acid is widely used in sodas and acidic foods like fruit juices and pickles. It is also used in chewing gum, candy, and cake mixes. A few studies have shown that ingestion of benzoic acid may cause hives, asthmatic attacks, and allergic reactions in children.

Both sodium benzoate and benzoic acid are chemically related to benzene, a known carcinogen, but slight changes in their chemical structure make them nontoxic, and in the eyes of the FDA they have been deemed to be safe for use. However, both sodium benzoate and benzoic acid may react with vitamin C in foods to form trace amounts of benzene. Therefore, it would make sense to avoid foods that are rich in vitamin C (like fruit juices) that have either sodium benzoate or benzoic acid added to them.

BHA (butylated hydroxyanisole) and *BHT (butylated hydroxytoluene)* are preservatives that are added to potato chips, breakfast cereals, and baked goods to prevent spoilage. Both have been shown to cause cancer in a variety of laboratory animals. And although humans are not lab rats, it would make sense to avoid eating too many foods with these additives in them, since we don't know their long-term negative effects.

Olestra (Olean): Olestra is a synthetic fat substitute that is used mostly in low-fat potato chips. Because it is not absorbed by the body, olestra passes quickly through the digestive tract, sometimes causing diarrhea and abdominal pain. In addition, olestra reduces the body's ability to take up certain vitamins (like beta-carotene), which need fat to be absorbed. There are some brands of low-fat chips that do not contain olestra, so be sure to check labels.

Potassium bromate: Potassium bromate is used to add texture and stability to flour. The body easily breaks it down during digestion, but small amounts of bromate may remain in foods and pose potential threats to health. Because bromate has been shown to cause cancer in lab animals, its use has been discontinued by many food producers; however, it is still found in a variety of baked goods.

Sodium nitrate and sodium nitrite: These are widely used as preservatives and flavoring agents in processed meats and lead to the formation of cancer-causing substances known as nitrosamines. Although the food industry is gradually decreasing their use, they can still be found in some brands of hot dogs, cold cuts, and bacon.

Artificial colors: Many artificial colors have already been banned by the government; however; various colorings are still widely used in soft drinks, candy, and baked goods. Artificial food coloring has been linked with a variety of health problems, including allergic reactions, hyperactivity in children, and certain cancers in lab animals. As with other risky additives, it makes sense to avoid eating large amounts of foods that have added food coloring.

Another food-related chemical to be aware of is bisphenol A (BPA). Although it is not used as an additive in foods, BPA is widely used in the manufacture of plastic water and soda bottles and microwavable food containers. Bisphenol A has been linked with a variety of health concerns, including increased risk of cancer, thyroid problems, and possible neurological problems, especially in infants and children.

BPA can leach or seep out of plastic packaging into foods and beverages, particularly at high temperatures such as those used in cooking. For this reason, it is a good idea to avoid heating foods in plastic containers and to limit consuming beverages bottled in plastics containing BPA.

Fortunately, many beverage manufacturers have discontinued using plastic bottles made with BPA and have begun to label those that still contain it. To know if a bottle has been made with a plastic that contains BPA, turn it upside down and check the number stamped on the bottom. Bottles marked with the number 7 are most likely to contain BPA.

Is Organic Better?

The explosion in the organic food movement in this country has been nothing short of astounding. In 1994, there were fewer than 3,000 organic farms in the United States. By 2007, there were 13,000. In addition, the organic food industry is growing 20 percent a year.

This tremendous interest and growth in the organic food industry can be linked to two main reasons: concern for the welfare and protection of the environment, and a desire on the part of consumers to eat clean, pure food free of chemicals and pesticides.

The concern about the toxins in our food is certainly legitimate. High levels of pesticides, heavy metals, and other synthetic chemicals have been found in grains, fruits and vegetables, nuts, and other crops. In addition, beef, poultry, and dairy products may contain high amounts of growth hormone and antibiotics, and seafood may be contaminated by the pollution found in the water. Pesticides and other synthetic chemicals can be highly poisonous, to both human health and the environment. Many studies have found that pesticides increase the risk of cancer, nervous system disorders, and serious hormonal imbalances. For a growing number of people, the possible risks presented by eating foods contaminated with pesticides and other chemicals are simply unacceptable, leading them to buy foods that have been organically grown.

Still, many people remain skeptical about the value of eating organically produced foods, since in many ways they are nutritionally equal to nonorganic foods. In addition, some people wonder if the term *organic* is legitimate—how can we be sure that foods labeled organic really are produced without any synthetic chemicals? Organic foods also tend to be more expensive, causing many people to wonder if the extra cost is justified.

People who doubt the legitimacy of the organic claim can rest assured that any food labeled organic must meet strict certification standards set by the USDA. The term *certified organic* means that a food has been produced without pesticides, hormones, antibiotics, irradiation, or genetically engineered ingredients. Organic farmers must undergo regular inspections to determine that they are complying with government regulations and must also follow practices that support soil and water conservation and the use of renewable resources. Organically grown foods are labeled with a special logo to inform consumers that they meet the strict production standards set out by the USDA.

Does it make financial sense to invest extra money in organic foods? This is a difficult question to answer, especially in the tough economic times we are experiencing. Certainly, eating a completely organic diet is beyond the budget of many people today. However, carefully picking and choosing which organic foods to buy might significantly lower your risk of ingesting pesticides, while being kind to your wallet.

Enter the group of foods known as the dirty dozen, a list of twelve fruits and vegetables known to contain the highest levels of pesticides. This list was developed by the Environmental Working Group (EWG), an agency that helps educate consumers about food, water, and environmental concerns. According to the EWG, eating the following twelve foods will expose a person to fifteen different pesticides:

- Celery
- Peaches
- Strawberries
- Apples
- Domestic blueberries
- Nectarines

- Bell peppers
- Spinach, kale, and collard greens
- Cherries
- Potatoes
- Imported grapes
- Lettuce

Choosing organic alternatives to the fruits and vegetables listed above represents a wise choice when it comes to spending your food dollars. However, if you cannot afford to buy organic, be sure to wash any foods on the dirty dozen list thoroughly to remove pesticide residues. A quick rinse is not enough to do this; you need to wash the food for several minutes under clean running water. And while careful washing will not remove all of the harmful pesticides, it will certainly help cut down on the amount left on the food.

In addition to the dirty dozen, the EWG has set up a list of "the clean fifteen"—fruits and vegetables with the lowest known amounts of pesticide residues. Because these foods have been given a clean bill of health when it comes to pesticides, buying organic forms of them is not a concern. Below are "the clean fifteen":

- Onion
- Avocado
- Sweet corn
- Pineapple
- Mango
- Sweet peas (frozen)
- Asparagus
- Kiwi
- Cabbage
- Eggplant
- Cantaloupe
- Watermelon
- Grapefruit
- Sweet potato
- Honeydew melon

In addition to lowering our exposure to pesticides, eating organic foods provides the advantage of helping to create a healthier environment. Cleaner soil, air, and water are benefits that will continue to have huge payoffs for years to come.

Negative Calories: Fact or Fiction?

Do you know about "negative calorie" foods—foods that supposedly burn more calories than they contain? Examples of these foods are fruits such as apples, grapefruit, and strawberries, and vegetables such as lettuce, broccoli, and cucumbers. According to the negative calorie theory, adding one or more of these foods to a high-calorie meal decreases the total calorie content of the meal. The reasoning behind this is the "thermic effect of food" (TEF)—the idea that digestion of these foods burns up more calories than they contain.

There is some scientific truth behind this theory, since some calories are used up or "wasted" when food is eaten. Although the reasons for this process are not clear, many nutrition researchers believe that digesting and absorbing food burns about 5 percent of the total calories eaten. Unfortunately, this thermic effect is not nearly enough to trigger weight loss, and like most things that sound too good to be true, the negative calorie theory of food is a myth. As an aside, fruits and vegetables offer many other benefits, including vitamins, minerals, powerful antioxidants, fiber, and water, and should be eaten in generous amounts, even if they don't help your body burn extra calories.

Meals and Snacks

The notion of eating "three squares" a day is part of American culture. Many of us grew up sitting down to breakfast, lunch, and dinner and never thought about skipping a meal. However, these days regular meals are a rare occurrence, due to the pressing demands of busy schedules, and many people now subsist on one meal a day, consisting of fast food or a frozen dinner. However, skipping meals is a poor nutritional practice that often leads to overeating and weight gain, as discussed on page xiv.

One of the most common reasons for skipping meals is lack of time. If this is a problem for you, consider stocking up on some portable foods that will help you eat on a more regular basis. And remember, breakfast, lunch, and dinner don't have to be traditional foods. It's perfectly okay to have a sandwich for breakfast and cereal for lunch! The idea is to eat a variety of foods regularly throughout the day to prevent extreme hunger and bingeing on junk foods.

Snacks count, too. Does this scenario sound familiar to you? It's 4:00 P.M. and you are at your desk, trying to fight the ravenous fog that is sweeping over you. Lunch seems as if it never happened, and you are craving a pick-me-up, probably sweet, maybe salty, perhaps both. All that stands between you and a dash to the vending machine or cafeteria snack bar is some dwindling self-control, and before you know it, you are munching down on a jumbo candy bar or a bag of chips. The funny thing is, after you finish eating it, you don't necessarily feel any more full or satisfied than you did before.

If this is your typical afternoon habit, welcome to the ranks of millions of Americans who routinely cave in to the lure of an afternoon snack. Don't get me wrong. There is absolutely nothing wrong with snacking—in fact, it can be a very healthy habit—it's our choices that get us into trouble. However, with a little bit of forethought and planning, we can learn to avoid the siren call of the candy machine and still satisfy our afternoon hunger pangs in a tasty and healthy way.

The first thing to check out when battling those afternoon cravings is the makeup of your lunch (assuming you ate it at all). If it followed a nonexistent breakfast and consisted of a Diet Coke and a salad of iceberg lettuce, you are well within your rights to be ravenous. So make sure your lunch is substantial enough to stick with you for more than an hour. It doesn't have to be large or fancy, but it should include 3 to 4 ounces of protein (tuna fish or cottage cheese on that salad or a lean roast beef sandwich will do nicely), so that you are genuinely full for 4 to 5 hours after you eat it.

Second, be prepared: Pack your own snacks and have them handy so you can avoid the trek to the vending machine. Fresh fruit is always a good choice; in addition, here are some other good snack choices:

- A cup of low-fat yogurt
- 1 to 2 ounces of peanuts or sunflower seeds
- 1 to 2 cups of popcorn (made with non-hydrogenated oils)
- 1 ounce of low-fat cheese with a handful of whole wheat crackers
- A small bag of honey-wheat pretzels
- A small bag of low-fat pita chips
- A cup of soup (yes, it makes a great snack!)

Food Safety

Any discussion of cooking at home would be incomplete without a mention of food safety. Believe it or not, food poisoning caused by improperly cooked or improperly handled food is skyrocketing in the United States, sometimes leading to hospitalization and more serious health conditions, even death. So to be safe when you cook, follow these guidelines:

Always wash your hands with soap and hot water before handling or cooking food.

Always cook meat, poultry, and pork thoroughly, until all traces of pink are gone. This is especially important for ground beef, which can be contaminated with dangerous E. coli bacteria. Thorough cooking helps destroy these nasty bugs. If you are unsure about how long to cook meat, invest in a meat thermometer and follow these temperature guidelines: Cook poultry and ground beef to 160° or 165°F, and other cuts of beef and pork to at least 145° or 150°F.

Cook eggs until their whites and yolks are firm, and never use eggs in a recipe unless they will be fully cooked.

Wash all cutting surfaces with soap and hot water. This is really important when you move from cutting meat to chopping vegetables—surfaces should be thoroughly cleaned each time to remove bacteria.

Keep hot foods hot and cold foods cold.

Refrigerate leftovers immediately. Allowing cooked food to sit at room temperature for even a short time is an invitation for bacteria to grow and cause serious illness.

Don't reuse sponges or dishcloths to clean countertops. These need to be laundered after each use to kill bacteria.

Don't thaw food by letting it sit outside the refrigerator. Instead, thaw it in the refrigerator, use the microwave (at defrost or medium setting), or submerge the food under cold running water.

The Obese Child

Few things are more troubling to a parent than watching a child struggle with a weight problem. From endless teasing at school to looming health problems, childhood overweight and obesity present difficult challenges to parents and families.

Though a detailed prescription for helping your overweight child is beyond the scope of this discussion, there are a variety of simple things you can do to help your child begin to move toward a healthy weight, while fostering a healthy self-image. First of all, it is important to remember the following:

Childhood obesity never occurs in a vacuum; it is always a family concern and needs to be treated as such.

Many factors play into a child's weight problem, ranging from family history to physical activity level to daily food habits. To focus on just one cause as a treatment option is to miss the whole picture and risk a poor chance of success.

Kids cannot and should not be expected to "diet." We already know diets don't work for adults, so why impose them on kids?

Keeping life "normal" is very important in trying to help your child lose weight. Making him or her "feel different" is a surefire way to fail.

Obesity and other weight issues do not develop overnight and do not have quick fixes. Patience is key!

Ways to Help Your Overweight Child

Below are some tips for helping your child work toward his or her healthy weight. These guidelines are by no means meant to replace the advice of a physician. *Always* consult your family doctor to make sure your child does not have any underlying health problems.

Don't use food as a reward or punishment, and *never* force your child to eat. In addition, allow small portions of favorite foods periodically, so that your child does not feel deprived.

It won't work to constantly restrict your child from snacking on chips, soda, and ice cream, while allowing other family members to eat them. Keep such tempting foods out of the house, and buy them as occasional treats.

Try to limit high-calorie take-out fare. Save the pizza for a Friday night once or twice a month instead of having it as a routine meal.

Whenever possible try to cook and eat dinner at home. This gives you one of the best opportunities to control the amount of calories, fat, and sugar you are putting on the table. Involve your child in meal preparation, and teach him or her about food. Kids love discovering new things, and learning about cooking and healthy eating is no exception.

Pack healthy snacks for lunch. Low-fat granola bars, yogurt, fruit or applesauce cups, and graham crackers are considerably lower in calories than candy bars and cookies, and most kids like them.

Involve your child's teacher, and let him or her know what you are trying to do. A teacher can keep an eye on what is happening in the lunchroom and at the vending machine.

Encourage outdoor play and exercise, no matter how limited. Even 15 minutes a day is better than nothing when it comes to burning calories and fostering healthy activity habits.

Don't compare your child's progress with that of other kids. Like adults, kids lose weight and become fit at different paces.

Be a great role model. All the talk and encouragement in the world is useless if you deliver it while munching on a Twinkie.

SOURCES

The nutritional information provided in this book was taken from the following sources:

USDA National Nutrient Database for Standard Reference, www.nal.usda.gov/fnic/foodcomp/search.

Corinne T. Netzer, *The Corinne T. Netzer Encyclopedia of Food Values* (New York: Delacorte Press, 1992).

TRADEMARKS

- Applebee's is a registered trademark of Applebee's International, Inc.
- Bahama Breeze is a registered trademark of Darden Concepts, Inc.
- Bennigan's is a registered trademark of Bennigan's Grill & Tavern, Bennigan's IP, LLC.
- Boston Market is a registered trademark of Boston Market Corporation, which is a wholly owned subsidiary of McDonald's Corporation.
- Buca di Beppo is a registered trademark of Planet Hollywood International, Inc.
- California Pizza Kitchen is a registered trademark of California Pizza Kitchen, Inc.
- Carrabba's is a registered trademark of OSI Restaurant Partners, LLC.
- The Cheesecake Factory is a registered trademark of The Cheesecake Factory, Inc.
- Chi-Chi's is a registered trademark of Chi-Chi's, Inc., and Prandium, Inc.
- Chili's is a registered trademark of Brinker International.
- Cracker Barrel is a registered trademark of CBOCS Properties, Inc.
- Daniel is a registered trademark of The Dinex Group.
- Dave and Buster's is a registered trademark of Dave & Buster's, Inc.
- Famous Dave's is a registered trademark of Famous Dave's of America, Inc.
- Golden Corral is a registered trademark of the Golden Corral Corporation.
- Hard Rock Cafe is a registered trademark of Hard Rock America, Inc.

- Hardee's is a registered trademark of Hardee's Food Systems, Inc.
- Houston's is a registered trademark of Bandera Restaurants.
- IHOP and International House of Pancakes are registered trademarks of International House of Pancakes, Inc.
- The Ivy is a registered trademark of Caprice Holdings, Ltd.
- Joe's Crab Shack is a registered trademark of Landry's Seafood Restaurants, Inc.
- KFC is a registered trademark of Yum! Brands, Inc.
- Luby's Cafeteria is a registered trademark of Luby's, Inc.
- Macaroni Grill is a registered trademark of Brinker International.
- Nobu is a registered trademark of Myriad Restaurant Group.
- O'Charley's is a registered trademark of O'Charley's, Inc.
- The Old Spaghetti Factory is a registered trademark of The Dussin Group.
- Olive Garden is a registered trademark of Darden Restaurants, Inc.
- Outback Steakhouse is a registered trademark of Outback Steakhouse, Inc.
- Panda Express is a registered trademark of Panda Restaurant Group, Inc.
- Panera Bread is a registered trademark of Panera Bread.
- P.F. Chang's China Bistro is a registered trademark of P.F. Chang's China Bistro, Inc.
- Planet Hollywood is a registered trademark of Planet Hollywood, Inc.
- Rainforest Cafe is a registered trademark of Landry's Restaurants, Inc.
- Red Lobster is a registered trademark of Darden Restaurants, Inc.
- Red Robin is a registered trademark of Red Robin International, Inc.
- Ruby Tuesday is a registered trademark of Morrison Restaurants, Inc.
- Sbarro is a registered trademark of Sbarro, Inc.
- Shoney's is a registered trademark of Shoney's, Inc.
- Steak and Ale is a registered trademark of Atalaya Capital Management.

- Texas Roadhouse is a registered trademark of Texas Roadhouse, Inc.
- T.G.I. Friday's is a registered trademark of T.G.I. Friday's, Inc.
- Union Pacific is a registered trademark of Main Street Restaurant Partners.
- Uno Chicago Grill is a registered trademark of Pizzeria Uno Corporation.
- White Barn Inn Restaurant is a registered trademark of US Hotels, Inc.

RESTAURANT WEB SITES

To find a restaurant near you, please visit:

Applebee's	www.applebees.com
Bahama Breeze	www.bahamabreeze.com
Bennigan's	www.bennigans.com
Boston Market	www.bostonmarket.com
Buca di Beppo	www.bucadibeppo.com
California Pizza Kitchen	www.cpk.com
Carrabba's Italian Grill	www.carrabbas.com
The Cheesecake Factory	www.thecheesecakefactory.com
Chi-Chi's	www.chichis.com
Chili's	www.chilis.com
Cracker Barrel	www.crackerbarrel.com
Daniel	www.danielnyc.com
Dave and Buster's	www.daveandbusters.com
Famous Dave's	www.famousdaves.com
Golden Corral	www.goldencorral.com
Hard Rock Cafe	www.hardrock.com
Hardee's	www.hardees.com
Houston's	www.hillstone.com
IHOP	www.ihop.com
The Ivy	www.the-ivy.co.uk
Joe's Crab Shack	www.joescrabshack.com
KFC	www.kfc.com
Luby's Cafeteria	www.lubys.com
Macaroni Grill	www.macaronigrill.com
Nobu	www.noburestaurants.com
O'Charley's	www.ocharleys.com
The Old Spaghetti Factory	www.osf.com
Olive Garden	www.olivegarden.com

Outback Steakhouse	www.outback.com
Panda Express	www.pandaexpress.com
Panera Bread	www.panerabread.com
P.F. Chang's China Bistro	www.pfchangs.com
Planet Hollywood	www.planethollywood.com
Rainforest Cafe	www.rainforestcafe.com
Red Lobster	www.redlobster.com
Red Robin	www.redrobin.com
Ruby Tuesday	www.rubytuesday.com
Sbarro	www.sbarro.com
Shoney's	www.shoneys.com
Texas Roadhouse	www.texasroadhouse.com
T.G.I. Friday's	www.fridays.com
Uno Chicago Grill	www.unos.com
White Barn Inn Restaurant	www.whitebarninn.com

INDEX

Gravy, Mushroom, Smothered Steak with, Luby's Cafeteria, 122–23
grilled:
    Baby Back Ribs, Chili's, 54–55
    Banzai Burger, Red Robin, 190–91
    Blue Mountain Chicken Sandwich, Rainforest Cafe, 185–86
    Bourbon Street Steak, Steak and Ale, 211
    Harvest Bay Mahimahi, Joe's Crab Shack, 115–16
    Hawaiian Chicken, Steak and Ale, 212
    Jamaican Jerk Chicken, Bahama Breeze, 15–16
    Margarita Chicken, Chili's, 59
    Salsa Verde Chicken Kabobs, Chi-Chi's, 50–51
    White Pekin Duck Breast, Union Pacific, 225–26

H

H. pylori, 251, 265
Harvest Bay Mahimahi, Joe's Crab Shack, 115–16
Hawaiian Chicken, Steak and Ale, 212
HDL cholesterol, 238, 239
heart arrhythmias, 238, 262
heartbeat, 241, 261, 262
heart disease, xiii, 233, 236, 238, 239, 241, 250, 253, 260, 261, 262, 269
herbal supplements, 258–59, 262–63
herbs, 250, 251
high blood pressure, xiii, 248, 250
high-fructose corn syrup, 233
home cooking:
    benefits of, xxiii–xxv, 232
    involving children in, xxiii, 279
honeydew melon, 274
hydrogenation, 239, 240
hydroxytyrosol, 250

I

Icing, Hardee's, 99–100
inflammation, 238, 250, 252
inflammatory bowel disease (IBD), 265
Insalata Florentina, Macaroni Grill, 132

iron, 268
irritable bowel syndrome (IBS), 243, 265
Italian:
    Chicken Crostina, Olive Garden, 147–48
    Chicken Saltimbocca, Buca di Beppo, 27–28
    Chicken Scaloppini, Macaroni Grill, 126–27
    Insalata Florentina, Macaroni Grill, 132
    Meat Loaf (Polpettone alla Montagona), Macaroni Grill, 135–36
    Risotto Milanese, Olive Garden, 157
    Sausage-Stuffed Portobello Mushrooms with Herb and Parmesan Cheese Sauce, Olive Garden, 153–54
    Tuscan Garlic Chicken, Olive Garden, 159–60
    see also pasta

J

Jamaican Jerk Grilled, Bahama Breeze, 15–16
Jambalaya Pasta, Cajun, The Cheesecake Factory, 40–41

K

Kabobs, Salsa Verde Chicken, Chi-Chi's, 50–51
kale, 274
kefir, 264
kidney disease, 248
kidney stones, 260
kiwi, 274

L

labels, reading, 239, 240
Lactobacillus, 264
lamb, in The Ivy Shepherd's Pie, 109–10
LDL cholesterol, 238, 239
leftovers, refrigerating, 278
legumes, 235
lemon:
    Butter, Chicken Francese with, Sbarro, 204–5
    Butter Sauce, Macaroni Grill, 126

Tex-Mex (*cont.*)
Chicken Quesadilla Grande, Applebee's, 3–4
Chicken Quesadillas, Ruby Tuesday, 196–97
Shrimp Fajitas, Hard Rock Cafe, 97–98
Steak and Mushroom Quesadillas, Chi-Chi's, 52–53
Steak Fajita Salad, Dave and Buster's, 77–78
thawing food, 278
theaflavins, 252
thermic effect of food (TEF), 275
tomato(es), 242
health benefits of, 251
Pico de Gallo, Applebee's, 11
Sun-Dried, Sauce, Carrabba's Italian Grill, 32
tortillas:
Baked Chicken Chimichangas, Chi-Chi's, 48–49
Beef Fajitas, Chili's, 56
Chicken Quesadilla Grande, Applebee's, 3–4
Chicken Quesadillas, Ruby Tuesday, 196–97
Shrimp Fajitas, Hard Rock Cafe, 97–98
Steak and Mushroom Quesadillas, Chi-Chi's, 52–53
Steak Fajita Salad, Dave and Buster's, 77–78
trans fats, 238–40
turkey:
Baked Monte Cristo Sandwich, Bennigan's, 19–20
sausage, *see* sausage (turkey)
turmeric, 251
Tuscan Garlic Chicken, Olive Garden, 159–60
tyrosol, 250

U

ulcers, 251, 265
unsaturated fat, 237
hydrogenated, 239
USDA, *see* Agriculture Department, U.S.
uterine cancer, 251
UV light, damage from, *251*

V

veal, in Carrabba's Italian Grill Meatballs, 34
vegans, 267, 268
vegetable(s), xiv, 231, 238, 240–42, 247
best choices, 242
Cheese Ravioli with, Olive Garden, 146
extracts, powdered, 259
fiber in, 243
health benefits of, 241–42
as low-GI foods, 253
nutrients in, 250
Stuffing, Boston Market, 25–26
typical serving of, 242
vegetable oils, 237
vegetarianism, 261, 267–69
vitamin A, 236, 241, 242, 258, 260
vitamin B$_{12}$, 268
vitamin C, 241, 258, 260, 270
vitamin D, 236, 258, 260, 261, 268
vitamin E, 236, 258, 260–61
vitamin K, 236
vitamins, 231, 250
fat-soluble, 236, 260
vitamin supplements, 258–62
Vodka, Rigatoni alla, Sbarro, 206

W

walnuts, 238
health benefits of, 250–51, 252, 253
Wasabi Butter Sauce, Shrimp, Oyster Mushrooms, and Sugar Snap Peas in, Nobu, 141–42
water, 245–47
drinking too much, 247
exercise and, 246, 247
in fruits and vegetables, 241
other fluids and, 247
recommended intake of, 245–46
watermelon, 255, 274
weight control, 233, 269
weight loss, xiv, 238, 241, 243, 253
high-protein diets for, 234, 235–36
wheat bran, 243